ABOUT THE AUTHOR . . .

ROBERT A. CLARK, M.D., Harvard-trained, did his psychiatric residency at Boston Psychopathic Hospital. He was three years on the staff of the Rhode Island State Hospital for Mental Diseases before coming in 1942 to the Western Psychiatric Institute and Clinics where he is Director of the Mental Health Clinic and Assistant Professor of Psychiatry, University of Pittsburgh School of Medicine.

During 1948-49 Dr. Clark was Rockefeller Fellow at the C. G. Jung Institute in Zurich. "Six Talks on Jung's Psychology" is a product of this study with the master himself, as well as of Dr. Clark's own research and practice.

C. G. JUNG'S Analytical Psychology merits more attention by American students and physicians, Dr. Clark maintains. Psychiatry is at an early stage of development. "We should think in terms of 'therapeutic pluralism,' not concentrating on any one doctrine ... but using whichever ... seems appropriate to the case under treatment." The Jungian theory is here presented without cultism or dogmatism. Dr. Clark finds in it a more adequate interpretation of some aspects of human behavior, and suggests that creative exchanges between Jungians and other "schools" will advance psychiatric science.

Churchmen will find SIX TALKS instructive reading; Jung respects the role of faith in effective living. Dr. Clark believes that Jung's Psychology has proved itself especially valuable in the treatment of patients, young and old, confronting spiritual difficulties or problems of conscience.

* * * *

SIX TALKS

ON

JUNG'S

PSYCHOLOGY

C. G. Jung.

SIX TALKS ON

Jung's Psychology

by Robert A. Clark, M.D.

Western Psychiatric Institute and Clinics

Pittsburgh, Pennsylvania

THE·BOXWOOD·PRESS

Pittsburgh 13, Pennsylvania

Drawings
by
CECILY HOGG

Lithoprinted in U. S. A.
by
EDWARDS BROTHERS, Inc.
Ann Arbor, Michigan

Preface

THE PERSON seeking help or the student wishing to learn may very well be confused by the different schools in psychiatry. He may ask: Why cannot those who claim to teach others how to live together, get along among themselves? He may conclude that all are mostly wrong and that everyone is just being misled and befuddled. He may reason that one school is all right and the others all wrong, that some share all the truth, or else that it is divided among all schools in different proportions. The outsider naturally thinks that where ideas conflict they cannot all be right.

It is my strong opinion that in a teaching institute for psychiatry, all of the different schools of thought should be given a fair hearing. That does not mean that one school is not better than another, nor that all schools are necessarily at the point where they deserve complete consideration. Nor do I believe that any particular school should be made the sole one taught at any teaching institute, at least in the present stage of psychiatry. We are in so early a stage of our development as a medical science that there is plenty of room for disagreement. Our data are not well measured and correlated when compared to that of the other medical sciences, so that it is possible to have a number of conflicting theories and still remain within the bounds of reason. We need to have a flexible outlook in psychopathology and psychotherapy. We should think in terms of "therapeutic pluralism," not concentrating on any one doctrine with fanatical intensity but using whichever one seems appropriate to the case under treatment.

At the present time the Freudian viewpoint is in the ascendant in many teaching centers for psychiatry. It would be unfortunate, in my opinion, if this led to the submergence of all other points of view. Any one school of thought lends itself to profitable development and application for an extended period of time. But in the long run the inspiration runs out and a sterile period sets in. The history of science shows that periodically the premises upon which a body of theory is built should be examined. New insights will then lead to new growth, often of a revolutionary depth and speed. We have seen this take place in physics within the last generation or two. The interchange of ideas between the two leading schools of Freud and Jung in psychiatric thought may stimulate both of them to new achievement. The road of isolation leads to cultism, with consequent dogmatism and rigidity.

This little book consists of materials that were presented, as a series of six lectures, to a group of physicians at the Western Psychiatric Institute and Clinics of the University of Pittsburgh.

I wish to express my gratitude and indebtedness to many persons. Henry A. Murray first introduced me to abnormal psychology and to Jung, and advised me to train in psychiatry. C. MacFie Campbell gave me my first teaching in clinical psychiatry. Grosvenor B. Pearson and Alan Gregg made it possible for me to study in Zurich. To Dr. Jung himself and to C. A. Meier and his colleagues at the Jung Institute, I owe most of my knowledge of analytical psychology. In this country, M. Esther Harding has guided my further studies. Lastly, colleagues and students too numerous to be mentioned by name have contributed to a productive interchange whose results will be evident to many of them in these pages.

Robert A. Clark

Western Psychiatric Institute and Clinics
Pittsburgh 13, Pennsylvania

Contents

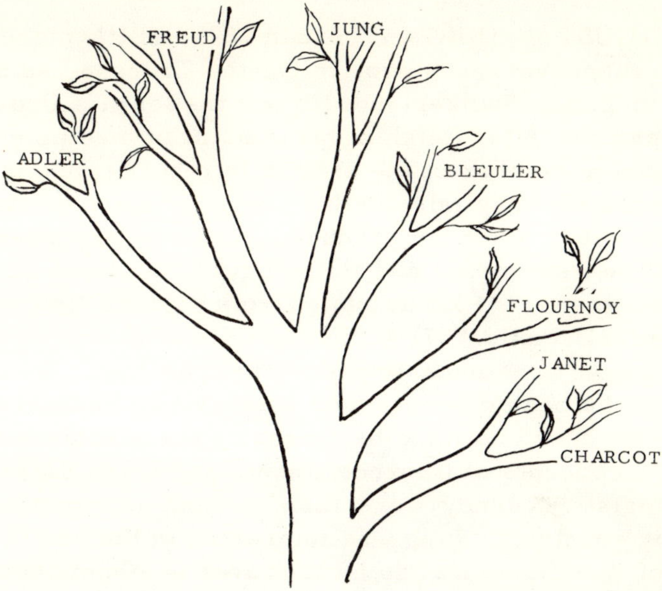

1

INTRODUCTION

JUNGIAN PSYCHOLOGY is considered by most people to be a branch of Freudian psychoanalysis. If so, it is a branch which has taken root and grown into a tree, but a tree so remote from America that few of us know much about it. There are a great many schools of psychotherapy; among others, the distributive analysis of Adolph Meyer; the client-centered therapy of Carl Rogers; Freudian psychoanalysis and its many offshoots; the functional approaches of Horney and of the Washington School; and Adlerian individual psychology. I have read the writings of members of many of these schools, and after sifting them all in my mind, have found particular appeal, because of my own temperament and interests, in the analytical psychology of C. G. Jung.

CARL GUSTAV JUNG was born in 1875, a little more than seventy-five years ago, in Canton Thurgau, as a citizen of Basle, Switzerland. He was the son of a Protestant pastor. After finishing his training in medicine, he became a member of the staff at Burghölzli, one of the psychiatric hospitals for the canton of Zurich. As early as 1902, when he produced his first published work, "The Psychology and Pathology of so-called Occult Phenomena," (13)* he quoted from Freud's "Interpretation of Dreams." (7) At that time Freud's doctrines did not make too much impression upon him. Soon afterward he became concerned with his own research into the unconscious mind by means of his association test. The concepts of Charcot, Janet, and of the Swiss psychologist Flournoy were then current in French-speaking countries. Jung was interested in the verification of their theories. So he took over an old method which had been developed by Galton, Aschaffenburg, and others in the previous twenty or thirty years. For the first time he used it to study the emotional character of the human mind rather than its intellectual structure alone.

From 1902 until about 1906, he was primarily concerned with this method of research. He was made Privat-Dozent (which corresponds to our title of assistant professor) in the University of Zurich's medical school. It was in 1906 that he realized that Freud's method of the study of dreams and their interpretation offered a still better method for the investigation of the unconscious than his own association test. He therefore went to see Freud. From the beginning their friendship grew. Freud recognized Jung's ability. Also he was delighted because this was the first recognition

*Numbers in parentheses refer to "References Cited" on page 78. A "Reading List" of books on Jung appears on page 81.

that he had received from orthodox psychiatry. He had previously been encouraged by the accession of a number of neurologists and scholarly laymen, but until that time his doctrines had been scorned by the psychiatrists attached to teaching institutions and medical schools.

With the support of Eugen Bleuler, who was then Professor of Psychiatry at the University and Director of Burghölzli, and with the help of many of the younger men in the Clinic, he proceeded for the first time to adapt Freud's ideas to the study of the psychoses. His book, "Psychology of Dementia Praecox"(15) is the product of that first period. It describes the application of his association test and psychoanalytic theory to the understanding of the disease now called schizophrenia. In 1909 he accompanied Freud on his trip to America, where Freud was recognized for the first time by academic psychologists. Jung also became the President of the International Psychoanalytical Association and managing editor of its journal of the time, the "Yearbook for Psychoanalytic and Psychopathological Research."* In his history of the psychoanalytic movement, Freud describes with great fairness, considering it was after he had broken with Jung, that he had even planned to transfer the headquarters of the movement to Zurich, then to retire into the background and to hand over the leadership to Jung. To Freud's great disappointment, this plan did not work out. Soon after the publication of Jung's first full-length book, "The Transformations and Symbols of the Libido," (translated into English as "Psychology of the Unconscious") (12) their friendship broke up. They had no further communication after 1913.

There were many differences between them,

*Jahrbuch für psychoanalytische und psychopathologische Forschungen.

both in technique and in theory. Jung always did have some reservations about Freud's ideas, even during the years when the two men were closely associated. In the introduction to the "Psychology of Dementia Praecox," Jung says, "I'm pleading for a fair hearing of Freud's ideas. If, I, for instance, recognize the complex mechanisms of dreams and hysteria, it by no means signifies that I ascribe to the infantile sexual trauma the exclusive importance seemingly attributed to it by Freud. Still less does it mean that I place sexuality so preponderantly in the foreground or that I even ascribe to it the psychological universality which Freud apparently postulates under the impression of the very powerful role which sexuality plays in the psyche. As for Freud's therapy, it is at best a possible one and perhaps does not always offer what one expects from it theoretically. Nevertheless, all these objections are quite incidental and completely vanish beside the psychological principles, the discovery of which is Freud's greatest merit, and to which the critics pay much too little attention." In the years before 1913, when he was closer to Freud, I suspect some of these reservations of his became much less prominent in his mind, but judging from what happened later, they were never completely dismissed.

Of the differences in technique in present-day practice, the most obvious, although by no means the most important, is that psychoanalysts have their patients lie on a couch and analytical psychologists do not. The first time I talked with Jung (in November, 1948), he spoke of this, saying that once Freud told him, "What do you expect me to do, have those people look at me all day long?" It is Jung's contention that to have a patient lie down on a couch places him in an inferior and subordinate position right from the beginning. Many neurotics like to be dependent, and to lie down merely encourages them in this need. Analytical psychologists feel that to have the patient sit on an equal level with the physician lets him see from the beginning that he is taking at least equal responsibility for his treatment. He is thus encouraged to stand on his own and carry his share of the responsibility. He can feel that the doctor respects his personality and intends to build up his ego rather than subordinate it.

Another difference is that between free association and what Jung has called amplification. Free association consists in following a train of thought from one idea to the next wherever it may lead. Amplification, as defined in Jolande Jacobi's "The Psychology of Jung," (10) is "a kind of limited, bound and directed association that returns ever and again to the center of significance given in the dream, revolving, as it were, about this very center." She says further, "Amplification illuminates all possible meanings for the dreamer in their contemporary present significance. Freud asks, 'Why?'; Jung asks above all, 'To what purpose?'." That is, instead of allowing the patient to go on by himself, the analytical psychologist keeps more control of the situation. If the patient seems to be wandering away, he feels it quite appropriate to bring him back to the original idea or image.

A more marked disagreement is with respect to the prospective function of dreams. The psychoanalytic approach to the dream is that it points to a present situation or to a past event in the patient's life. In the 1912 number of the Jahrbuch, there appeared an article by Alphonse Maeder, a Swiss psychiatrist and colleague of Jung's, entitled "Concerning the Function of Dreams." (19) It was there first brought out that a dream may refer to future as well as present or past events. I will quote Maeder, himself. "In many dreams of healthy and sick people tendencies are demonstrable, which constellate for the first time the subsequent manifest behavior and thinking of the dreamer. Many dreams act like preparatory exercises or readying for later waking activity; they seek and give attempts at solution of existing actual conflicts; they create a sort of pathway in the confusion of our contradictory impulses. . . A similar biological function is well known to us, that of play."(19) This concept became part of the doctrine of the Zurich school. Freud and most of his colleagues in Vienna found it impossible to accept this viewpoint.

The differences in theory I can only hint at now. In later talks I hope to go into some of them more thoroughly. I refer briefly to them now just as a preliminary background.

LIBIDO THEORY

JUNG DISTINGUISHES between what he calls the objective and the subjective approach to the psyche. He says, for example, that if a person dreams about anyone who is important to his emotional life: a close relative or friend, then the dream refers to that objective relationship and should be so interpreted. However, if a figure appears in the dream whom the dreamer does not know, or to whom he is not closely related emotionally, then it has a subjective meaning. This implies that it refers to something unconscious within the person's own psyche. It may be either a repressed tendency, or a potentiality in his psyche which has never been conscious, although it could be something in the future. It is also true that a figure in a dream or phantasy which seems objective may have a subjective interpretation in addition. This would appear to be unnecessarily complicating matters. It is often hard enough to track down what a dream may mean in terms of the person's present or past life, without introducing something new. It might be said, too, that this subjective interpretation has its pitfalls, that it is possible for an enthusiastic analytical psychologist, full of the subjective viewpoint expressed in legends, myths, and rituals, to pay insufficient attention to the objective life of the patient, and run off to the happy hunting ground of the inner life. The analytical psychologist, on the other hand, can equally criticize the psychoanalyst for sticking too closely to the patient's present and past life and not paying enough attention to future potentialities. It is often these potentialities which will lead to improvement or cure rather than what he has experienced in the past. Here, again, we have an idea which is not peculiar to Jung. Herbert Silberer was a colleague of Freud's in Vienna in his early days, one of the most brilliant of his followers. Unfortunately, he died in the first World War while serving in the Medical Corps of the Austrian Army. In his book, "Problems of Mysticism and its Symbolism,"(21), he indicates that the obscure symbols of alchemy can be understood in three ways: the psychoanalytic, leading to the depths of the impulsive life; the hermetic, leading to the higher ideals; and the ethically indifferent or "chemical." He contrasts the first approach with the second, which he calls the "anagogic," pointing to potentialities for the further development of the personality, along ideal as well as practical lines.

Another difference in theory is that of the <u>reductive</u> versus the <u>constructive</u> approach. The former analyzes the patient's dreams and phantasies in terms of his past life while the latter uses them to anticipate a future and better integrated personality. This can be illustrated by a dream a patient once reported. This man, forty years of age, had a problem in his sexual life and also was very immature in his general psychologic development. He was single, still living with his parents, unable to tear himself away from dependence upon them. The high point of the dream was that the patient found he had the end of his own penis in his mouth. He was enjoying the experience, had an orgasm, but there was no nocturnal emission. I presume the psychoanalytic interpretation of this dream would be that the patient was an extreme narcissist.

I think that this is a correct interpretation, but not the only one. There are at least two other ways of looking at it: one, that it represents the beginning of the patient's attempt to accept his own sexuality by uniting the upper and lower halves of the body. It is traditional in our society that the upper part of the body, including the head and the heart and lungs, is the "purer" part, and the lower part which contains the excretory and sexual organs, is considered to be "impure." At the second (or anagogic) level, the dream looks toward the future. The patient seems to be fertilizing himself. The sex relation is primarily an act of fertilization. By having, as it were, sexual relations with himself, he may become "pregnant" and "give birth" to a child, namely a new and more mature personality. He can develop psychosexually, tear himself away from his dependence upon his parent and become an adult whose behavior suits his age.

Jung's concept of the libido, or psychic energy, as he prefers to call it, differs considerably from that of Freud's. It is much more general and more philosophical, not strictly biological. As noted in the introduction to the "Psychology of Dementia Praecox," he places much less emphasis upon sex than Freud did when the latter's outlook was still strictly sexual, in the dictionary definition of the word.

Last, there is the theory of a deeper level of the unconscious, far below that which psychoanalysts recognize. Along with Freud, Jung realized that psychic material which has already been in consciousness, or at least has struggled to get over the threshold of consciousness, can be repressed into the unconscious. But he felt that this material constituted only the personal unconscious of the individual—a product of his experience in his own life. He became convinced, from experiences with his patients, that there was a still deeper level, which he called the collective unconscious. A most succinct definition of this term is this: "The collective unconscious is an inheritance of the possibility of ideas." Note the word "inheritance." Jung was a clinical psychiatrist brought up in the tradition of German and French psychiatry, which emphasized at that time the great importance of hereditary factors in the development of the mind. Psychoanalysis was a revolt against that outlook, then very much needed. Typical of the Freudian view was that of A. A. Brill, published in a paper in 1912, that at birth the mind was a tabula rasa—a clean slate (2). Jung's concept of the unconscious is an attempt to bring together the factor of inheritance on the one hand and that of personal experience on the other. The mind is considered to be the product of, or the correlate of, the activity of the brain. We recognize that the rest of the body owes its form largely to hereditary factors. It was Jung's contention that the structure of the brain, although it cannot be observed directly, has the same characteristic. He went a step further when he said that many of the ideas and images which come out of our brains are inherited not only in terms of one's own family but also in terms of the human race as a whole. He emphasized, first, the resemblances between the brains of all human beings rather than the possible differences among men of different races and cultures.

He used several lines of evidence to support this idea. When he studied the mythology of primitive races, in order to understand the strange dreams which so many patients brought to him, he was struck by the many resemblances in myths and tales despite the geographical remoteness of the peoples creating them. One might argue that they had learned the myths from each other, but that seems very unlikely, considering the poor methods of transportation which these people had. We might suppose in the case of the American Indians, that they originally came, according to anthropological theory, from the continent of Asia, and preserved the same myths through hundreds of generations. Although it is possible to believe this theory, it seems at least equally tenable that the reason these people produce the same sort of myths is because they have the same kind of brain. That is, the possibility of producing the same general ideas is resident in each human brain no matter where it lives or in what age.

Jung also found that many of his patients, knowing nothing of the legends or religious symbols of remote tribes and civilizations, modern materialists whose minds were seemingly filled only with scientific facts or how to make the most money in their short lives, dreamed in symbols found only in remote regions or times—remote not only geographically but historically. Consequently, he felt that the hypothesis of the collective unconscious was necessary to explain these remarkable similarities. In addition, he found archaic and primitive images in the delusions and hallucinations of his schizophrenic patients.

In spite of all their differences, the psychoanalytical and the analytical psychological schools still hold many things in common. Both believe in the importance of individual analysis for the patient; and of personal analysis for the candidate for training. Both believe in the importance of the interpretation of dreams; both hold to the fundamental theory of the existence of an unconscious mind. In thinking of eventual reconciliation of these two schools of thought, I might refer to a quotation of Freud's which he wrote before the break took place. It is from a postscript he wrote to a published case, that of Schreber, and can be found in the third volume of his "Collected Papers."(4). "This short postscript on the analysis of a paranoid patient may serve to show that Jung had excellent grounds for his assertion that the myth-making forces of mankind are not extinct but that to this very day, they give rise in the neuroses to the same psychological products as in the remotest past ages. I should like to take up a suggestion that I, myself, made some time ago, and add that the same holds good of the forces that work for the formation of religions. And I am of the opinion that the time will soon be ripe for us to make an extension of a principle of which the truth has long been recognized by psychoanalysts, and to complete what has hitherto had only an individual and ontogenetic application by the addition of its anthropological and phylogenetically conceived counterpart. 'In dreams and in neuroses,' so our principle has run, we come once more upon the child and the peculiarities which characterize his modes of thought and his emotional life,' and 'we come upon the savage, too,' thus we may complete our proposition, 'upon the primitive man, as he stands revealed to us in the light of the researches of archaeology and of ethnology.'"(4). When the break took place Freud dropped this possible way of reconciliation. A bit from his "History of the Psychoanalytic Movement," (3) shows how far away from Jung he was even a short time later. "Jung's modification is so unintelligible, obscure, and confused that it is difficult to take up any standpoint in regard to it. Wherever one lays hold of anything, one must be prepared to hear that one has misunderstood it, and it is impossible to know how to arrive at a correct understanding of it." Freud later on, in his "Totem and Taboo," (5) followed up this anthropological, phylogenetic trend somewhat but nowhere did he develop it to the extent to which it has been done by Jung and his followers.

Jung has expounded his libido theory in various writings. The primary source for what follows is the essay "On Psychical Energy," found in "Contributions to Analytical Psychology."(14). Psychical energy, he says, derives its source from the nerve cells of the cerebrum. It owes its particular expression to the form and relationship of these millions of cells in the human brain. Jung speaks of the conservation of psychical energy as analogous to the conservation of physical energy. The mind is a closed system no more than temporarily because it is continually subject to influxes from the outside as well as expressing itself toward the outer world. But certainly for the more civilized portion of humanity, activities entirely within the brain take a very large proportion of cerebral energy. As the organism lives its life, if things go smoothly, it tends to express its psychical energy in a progressive manner. If we imagine the unfrustrated human life as a flat surface, the progression of psychical energy might be compared to a stream entering upon the surface and gradually spreading over it, much as water breaking through a dam begins to spread over fields which had previously been dry. If this orderly and gradual process is interfered with because the environment is not suitable, or because the psyche attempts some method of adaptation which is not appropriate to the environment in which it finds itself, this flow is dammed up and repression takes place. With this repression there is a certain amount of dissociation in the mind because usually the ego finds itself able to progress in some directions but not in others. If the damming up is sufficiently extensive, actual regression will take place to earlier methods of adaptation. So far, this description is common to that of psychoanalysis.

Jung uses the terms "evolution" and "involution" to describe what may happen in some minds in order to overcome this damming back. The natural tendency of human minds is not to develop as though on a flat surface but to grow upwards and to have different methods of adaptation at different times of life. This growth is to a large extent synchronized with the different periods of life: childhood, adolescence, adulthood, the climacteric and old age. Each age of life requires a different method of progression. That which is suitable to one level of life, may not be suitable for another. A constant series of such evolutionary changes should go on in each individual life. The person who is making progress toward maturity advances in steps – first over one surface and then rising to a new step with its new surface, and so on. If this evolutionary progress is interfered with, he will have a feeling of frustration and dissatisfaction and may resort to involution before attempting the next step upward. In other words, to step upward, he must first step down. He must go down to the lower levels of mind, into the personal or even to the collective unconscious and find some of his potentialities for further development and action which he has not called upon before. While he was progressing or evolving normally, there was no need to call on these potentialities which may have had no place in his culture. Therefore he may have to bring up something unheard of in that civilization in order to grow to a higher stage of psychological evolution. If he is acting unconsciously, this involution may show itself in the form of a neurosis or a psychosis, which brings up primitive material that is very disturbing to the ego. If the person is undergoing analysis, this same process may be gone through purposely, with the guidance of the analyst. In these terms if psychoanalysis can be called a purposeful neurosis, Jungian analysis could be characterized as a purposeful schizophrenia.

In the physical world, the transmission of energy depends a great deal upon contrast between the objects concerned–for example, if a person has a hot object in one hand and a cold one in the other, there will be an energy exchange in the form of heat. So, in the human mind, when there is a contrast existing between progression and regression, between evolution or involution, between good and evil, sadism and masochism, passivity and aggressiveness, or any pair of opposites of which we can think–then a tendency for transmission of psychical energy is present. The person works within himself or in the outer world and tries to bring about a reconciliation between the opposites. If this process were to go on undisturbed, one would, I suppose, come to an end point corresponding to what the physicist calls entropy, expressed in the second law of thermodynamics. In the human mind, since it is not a closed system, this leveling process very soon comes to an end. Only a dilapidated schizophrenic could be said to have reached such a stage because he has withdrawn himself from further stimulation by the outer world. To designate this interplay between the opposites, Jung uses a technical term borrowed from the Greek philosopher Heraclitus: enantiodromia.

In order for evolution to take place, the psyche uses means of transforming its energy. "Transformation of libido (corresponding to transformation of physical energy) occurs through its transference to an analogue of the object of an instinct, as in the case of primitives who have sex relations in a field in Spring to encourage germination and agriculture. Rites d'entree and baptismal and dedication ceremonies have similar aims. The psychological machine which transforms energy is the symbol. Only where a symbol offers a greater potential than nature, can libido be converted into other forms. Not all is bound up in natural flow but some (the excess libido) remains over. Symbols are the manifestation and expression of this excess libido, and transitions to new cultural activities, in contrast to instinctive functions. Symbols are never thought out consciously; they are produced from the unconscious by "revelation," or intuition. Probably many historical symbols arose from or were inspired by dreams. In the course of time there is a tendency toward the suppression of individual symbols—for example, by the establishment of a state religion. We may anticipate a renewal of individual symbol-formation." (14) That is, most people, in the course of their individual development, make use of established symbols such as are offered by the culture in which they live. But in a rapidly changing culture such as ours, these traditional symbols, whether they are those of religion or nationalism, tend to lose their force. In fact, for an individual to develop to higher levels of psychological evolution nowadays, he often has to make his personal interpretation of traditional symbols or discover new ones of his own in the collective unconscious.

In the manner just described, an individual can develop through the three stages of his life: childhood, a naive stage of development, similar to that of primitive man; adolescence and early adulthood, corresponding to a stage of sophistication in which the individual is learning to find his place in the world into which he is born; and the third stage, (called by Jung "the second half of life") which most of us put off as long as we can, but which he insists is an essential part of individual development. Jung seeks to aid people to develop self-understanding in terms of their inner lives throughout later adulthood and the climacteric. The period of physical involution may thus become one of continued active psychological growth.

This whole process Jung calls individuation. He defines it as "the psychological process that makes a human being an 'individual'—a unique, indivisible unit or 'whole man.'" (16). "Wherever the cultural process is moving forward the disintegration of collective convictions is to be found. An advance always begins with individuation—through the fact that an individual, conscious of his uniqueness, cuts a new way through untrodden country." (14)

As the ego develops, it grows a shell around it, known as the persona. This was the name given to the mask worn by ancient classical actors in Greek and Roman times. We all learn to wear such a persona in order to show toward the outer world only that part of ourselves which we feel it wishes to see. The persona has two functions. The first is protective; that is, in order for consciousness and awareness of one's self to arise, the growing ego must be protected from overwhelming influences from the outside. In this fashion, it is able to develop a certain degree of individuality. Just as the masks of classical times had eye holes and mouth holes, so that the actors could see and talk to each other and with the audience, the persona has also a communicative function. It permits the ego to exploit the outside world for its own interests. The persona develops to a variable degree in different people. Some of us develop little or none. We call many such people psychopathic personalities, or, to use a newer term, neurotic characters. They may have little conscious awareness, either of themselves or of others. They can, on the other hand, be very sensitive to everything from the outside world and be continually in turmoil because they cannot protect themselves from it. It may be true in other people that the persona is poorly adapted to the environment. Perhaps the ego has worked very hard to develop a persona which it may think to be an excellent one, but to the eyes of the outside observer, it is not at all well adapted. The ego may identify itself with some ideal image which has been presented to it by its society. For example, we at times see physicians with a bedside manner which is so artificial that it is almost ridiculous. A politician may cut an obviously insincere figure which is very easy to caricature. Such people are often referred to as "stuffed shirts." That is, they have personas, but very little genuine adaptation or very little adequately individuated personality within to fill them out. Another possibility is that a man who has made a great success of persona development may be carried away by it. He identifies himself very closely with some institution for which he works or some office that he holds. His persona then becomes puffed up much larger than the resources of his personality justify. This is called the inflation of the persona. I suppose that many of the people around Hitler, who were actually carried away by the Nazi doctrines, not consciously exploiting them as Hermann Goering probably was, were inflated in this manner. They so identified themselves with their vision of the spirit of German nationalism that they lost all perspective of their position in the eyes of the rest of the world. One continually sees less exaggerated degrees of such inflation. People identify themselves, for example, with a church, with their profession, or perhaps with a school of psychotherapy such as psychoanalysis, even analytical psychology. In any case, they become very dogmatic and no longer recognize their own personal limitations. The persona can nevertheless be a very useful part of the personality. But it is subject to over- or under-development so that difficulties may arise which are not pathological in the psychiatric sense but which certainly interfere with the smooth functioning of society.

In addition to growing a persona, the child must develop a protection against irruptions from the collective unconscious. Children often have nightmares, perhaps because this barrier against the unconscious is not highly enough developed. As the adult personality appears, the nightmares no longer occur. For those who wish to know about Jungian child psychology and psychiatry, I recommend to you two books in the "Reading List": "The Inner World of Childhood" by Frances Wickes of New York and "The Life of Childhood" by Michael Fordham of London. I shall not say more about the early development of the personality but go on to a description of Jung's psychological types, an important part of his ego psychology.

The best known of all Jung's concepts are the two psychological attitudes: extraversion and introversion, These terms are so familiar that most people do not know that Jung invented them. The extravert is interested in objects and personalities outside his own ego. The introvert, on the other hand, is mainly concerned with his inner life; consequently his attention is directed toward that which comes from the unconscious. Here we have an example of enantiodromia, that is, interplay between opposites. No one is completely extraverted nor completely introverted. Every extravert has his introverted side and vice versa. The side which he does not express is relatively under-developed or repressed and remains in an undifferentiated or comparatively primitive state.

Jung also speaks of the four functions of the personality. It is curious that so many psychologists, who are well acquainted with the attitudes of extraversion and introversion, seem to be completely unaware of the functions, though it is inappropriate to speak of one without including the others as well. The functions are capacities of the personality which may be differentiated to varying degrees. Jung divides them into two pairs: first, those with which the person becomes aware of the environment or of the inner world: second, those with which he elaborates the data so acquired. The one best known to us is that of sensation. Through it a person is able to observe closely the events around and within him, to elaborate them so that they can be classified in his mind and reported to others. A person with a highly developed sensation function can be, among other things, an excellent natural scientist, because he is able to observe accurately those data presented to his senses and to describe and report them adequately. He might just as well be an excellent mechanic or farmer.

I have been speaking so far of the extraverted sensation type. Each function expresses itself through the attitude which is natural to that personality. An introverted sensation type is better able to observe his inner life. If he were a psychologist, for example, he would be a good introspectionist and be able to report very well the subjective side of both sensations and emotional responses. If he were a novelist, he would be able to describe accurately the perceptions and feelings of his characters.

We are less aware of intuition as a way of knowing about the external and the internal worlds. At least in our culture, which emphasizes learning through sensation, it is more in the unconscious. Intuition shows us the outer world through those impressions which we cannot describe clearly but still are there–for example, the facial expressions and gestures continually used by the people around us. Intuition records its observations in generalities rather than in particulars. These subjective impressions arrange themselves into general impressions on the borderline of consciousness before the ego becomes aware of them. These impressions appear in clear consciousness as though already made. We do not know just where they came from, but nevertheless, for people who trust their intuitions, they have the same validity as sensations. From the inner world still more is derived by intuition. People do not habitually observe their emotions. Rather do they appeal to them intuitively without asking themselves where they come from. In doing so they are exercising the introverted intuitive function.

Sensation and intuition contrast with the functions of thinking and feeling. Thinking takes the data offered to it by sensation and intuition, and classifies it according to natural logical categories. The feeling function is the most difficult to understand, at least for Westerners. It is perhaps better denoted by the term evaluating, because it is concerned with the classification of external or internal data supplied through sensation and intuition in terms of liking and disliking, pleasantness and unpleasantness, and arranging them into a hierarchy of values. While using the thinking function, feelings and emotions are excluded as much as possible. That is why the scientist tries to be as cold and as unemotional as he can be in observing facts and in constructing theories. In using the feeling function, however, the door must be left open to the feelings and emotions. Otherwise, there would be no data for this function to work with. The extraverted thinking person is mainly concerned with adaptation to the outer world and exploitation of it. He may be a theoretical scientist, like Darwin, for example, who was not primarily concerned with the collection of scientific facts, although he may be superior in that too. His main interest is in constructing a theory which makes logical order out of those facts. An introverted thinker may become a mathematician or a philosopher. I believe it was William Hamilton, the great Irish mathematician, who, when he invented the theory of quaternions in the middle of the 19th century, was very pleased because it had no practical application. The theory appealed to him because of its beauty. The philosopher also is usually little concerned with the application of his ideas in the outer world.

The extraverted feeling type is mainly interested in relationships with those about him. The feeling introvert, on the other hand, is mainly occupied with the evaluation of his own feelings. He may make an excellent modern artist or novelist. James Joyce was primarily concerned with expressing his own feelings and evaluations. He did not care, I presume, whether anyone reading his "Ulysses" understood it or not.

Jung divides the functional types into the irrational and rational. Sensation and intuition are irrational in the sense of being non-rational or empirical. They merely report data. Thinking and feeling, however, are both considered as rational. We are apt to think that only the thinking function is a rational one, but to Jung evaluating is equally so. This rational use of feeling

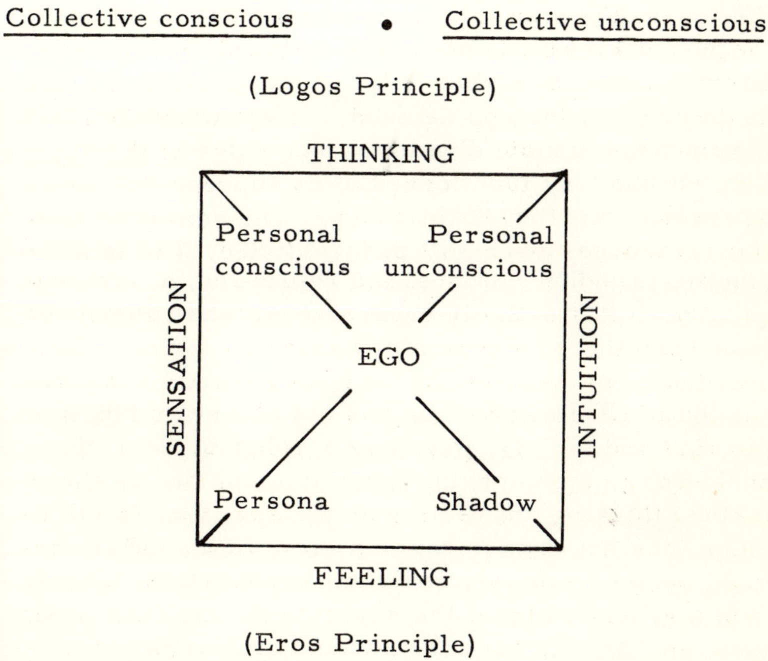

Figure 1. The psychological functions. Thinking and feeling are always opposite sensation and intuition.

might be demonstrated by a theologian, who is concerned that the results of this thinking have value, that is, meaning for the conduct of individuals and for the organization of society.

Certain functions may be more developed in one person and less developed in another. Let me refer to Figure 1 for a moment. On the left we have the collective conscious, on the right the collective unconscious. The region between them, in the infant mind, might be represented by a dot in the center with no dividing line whatsoever. As the child develops a dividing line begins, becoming more prolonged as the persona develops toward the collective conscious. Portions of this side of the square are open for communication. It is as though the persona were made like a venetian blind rather than an ordinary window shade. It can be opened and closed as the needs of the ego demand, except when the cords get stuck and trouble develops. The sides of the square indicate the four functions. Let us suppose that this is a personality of the sensation type. The sensation function is then the most highly differentiated. The intuitive function is undifferentiated and repressed, and is consequently almost entirely unconscious. The subject may be an excellent observer of the external world or of his own inner experiences, but he is able to use his intuition hardly at all. However, he has his other two functions, thinking and feeling, partially developed. Sensation is spoken of as the superior function, intuition as the inferior, thinking and feeling as the auxiliary functions. Since it is not easy to develop three functions at once, most people have only one auxiliary function. There is then a gradation from the superior to the first auxiliary function, through the second auxiliary, to the inferior. One can, therefore, speak of the sensation-thinking or of the sensation-feeling type. Similarly, the person who is primarily a thinking type may have either sensation or intuition as his auxiliary function.

One might ask: "From whence do the attitudes and functions arise?." Fundamentally, they originate constitutionally. We do not know just how, any more than we know very much about the hereditary or constitutional factors in most of the human body, particularly in the nervous system. So far as Jung can tell us from his observations of his patients and others he has studied, people are born with a capacity to differentiate one attitude or function better than the others. Because of a certain amount of elasticity, cultural factors enter in as well. If a person who is naturally an introvert is born into a family where business or natural science holds the field, he will try to develop his extraverted side. This may cause considerable strain resulting in poor differentiation of the persona, perhaps in neurotic symptoms as well. Conversely, an extraverted person born into a family of artists primarily concerned with emotional values would run into a similar difficulty in the opposite direction. It is also possible for a person to develop his leading or superior function to such a high degree that his other functions are almost entirely ignored. In that case the personality will be lopsided. He may become a very skillful mechanic, successful professional man or clever intellectual, but he will be maladjusted or internally dissatisfied because his personality is so inharmonious.

From his observation of dreams and fantasies, Jung has theorized that these attitudes and functions, as well as the persona, may be represented in various ways. In the dream, the ego complex is represented by the dreamer. His persona may be shown as a suit of clothes. If the persona is poorly developed, the ego may be represented as partially or completely nude. If his persona is poorly adapted to the environment, he may dream that he is dressed in some ridiculous and embarrassing costume. If he needs a new persona, he will be trying on new clothes or having his old suit remodelled.

The functions can appear in dreams as colors in association with the classical elements. Sensation may be suggested by green—usually associated with the earth, as it is customarily covered by grass and leaves. Intuition may be represented by yellow or white, associated with water. When something is brought up from below the surface, it cannot be seen until it is on top. The thinking function is implied by blue, suggesting the sky and the air. Thinking, when over-differentiated, often loses contact with the earth. Feeling may be represented by red or by fire. So we have the four primary colors and the four elements as often conceived by the ancients and the alchemists.

Two other concepts have been introduced more recently by Jung in his discussion of the psychology of the sexes. Persons, most commonly men, who take data from sensation and intuition and use them mainly through the thinking function are said to be exercising the Logos principle. Since feeling is par excellence the function of value relations, the person exercising the Eros principle, most often a woman, is mainly interested in personal relationships. There are many exceptions, but that is the usual situation as Jung has observed it. Here, again, we have a contrast between opposites. If a person's Logos principle is highly developed, his Eros principle is relatively undifferentiated and vice versa.

3

HOW WE KNOW THE UNCONSCIOUS. THE SHADOW

THE UNCONSCIOUS covers so vast a territory, and has such unplumbed depths, that it rather naturally lends itself to verbal comparisons with the seas, whose vastnesses harbor creatures no more bizarre than those that can be dredged up from the sea of the unconscious. Before sending down our dredging equipment, let us first consider the viewpoint we have to take before we can begin to understand the materials brought up by our exploration of the unconscious.

I have already described the two attitudes—extraversion and introversion—and the four functions in relation to the attitudes. In our extraverted society the sensation function is ordinarily turned toward the outer world. Those with a scientific education like to think that they are especially trained to observe the outer world carefully in order not to be subject to illusions due to the interference of emotions or prejudices. But they are not so accustomed to turning their sensation function inwards and observing the inner world. The academic psychologist does this to a certain degree when he practices introspection in the psychological laboratory. Psychotherapists encourage their patients to study their own feelings, emotions and dreams so that they may understand themselves better. But the average psychiatrist still thinks in terms of the adjustment of the patient to the outer world.

Jung has spent more time than the average present-day psychiatrist concentrating upon the inner aspect of our consciousness. For forty years or so, he has been collecting all kinds of data from many sources of information concerning the unconscious. The first few familiar ones he puts similar value upon as do psychoanalysts and other depth psychologists. Slips of speech and action allow us to gain knowledge of emotional complexes near to the surface of consciousness. Daydreams are usually either wishfulfilling or express feelings of aggression. Jung places as much stress upon dreams as do psychoanalysts, but he looks at them with a somewhat different viewpoint. He divides dreams into two main varieties. First are those common ones which do not disturb us particularly. We may find them amusing and recount them at the breakfast table, or they may be so colorless that we soon forget them. These merely reflect experiences of the day before in a compensatory way. They may give some clues to the upper layers of the unconscious.

The second category of dreams is much more striking and presumably more significant. Anxiety dreams, which are filled with fearful and aggressive images, directed against the ego, often result in the dreamer awakening in a panic. These dreams point to the deeper layer of the personal unconscious. There are also the so-called "big" or cosmic dreams, more mythological and accompanied by a feeling of awe, as though something very important and dramatic were being enacted. Often they are expressed in abstract, general terms, with little or no reference to the personal life of the dreamer.

Anxiety dreams are apt to be remembered much more clearly than the every-day dreams. The big dreams may be remembered for years as mile-stones in the inner experience of the dreamer. I have a friend, not a patient, who once described to me some dreams of this sort which she had had about ten years earlier. They affected her so much that ten years later she was able to sit down without notes and type them out. They have had a great effect upon her conscious life.

In the course of analysis, the analytical psychologist makes much more use of drawings and paintings than most other psychotherapists, who are accustomed to using drawings a great deal in treating children but not adults. The analytical psychologist feels that he gets genuine insight into the unconscious through drawings. I do not mean landscapes or portraits, but rather spontaneous, or "unconscious" drawings, produced when a person sits down and draws whatever comes into his head. If you go to a contemporary art exhibit you will find a great many paintings by modern artists which seem quite incomprehensible to the average conservative citizen, who is apt to wonder why on earth they hang those things on the wall anyway. But to a Jungian analyst, many such productions are truly spontaneous and potential mines of information concerning the unconscious of the artists. The patient or the student in training is encouraged to make such drawings, whether he has any artistic ability or not. It is better if he does not have any training, because then he is less apt to be diverted from spontaneity by what he has learned in art school.

Anxiety dreams reach down into the personal unconscious, while the cosmic dreams plumb the collective unconscious. Drawing and painting help to bridge the gap between the two as daydreams do. Another function of artistic work is to help fix dream material so that the person can think of it as more real, associate to it more readily and consequently make more use of it in his analysis. Dreams tend to be fleeting, even if written down, because in words they do not seem as real as when they are painted vividly. Oftentimes one encourages the patient or student to draw what he has seen in his dream and then develop other drawings from the first as his fancy leads him on.

Other types of inner experience which the patient may report are hypnagogic and hypnopompic visions. It is true they are not so frequent as the other experiences I have mentioned, but when they do occur they may be valuable. These are visions or hallucinations which occur in a half-waking, half-sleeping state–the hypnagogic, on going to sleep, and the hypnopompic on waking up. They are often vivid and anxiety-producing. I have a patient, for example, who tells me that many times he will half wake up and be able to see his room dimly around him, but as though the windows and doors were far away so that he has difficulty placing them. It gives him a great feeling of strangeness and insecurity. He is a very insecure man, who is having a hard time finding his place in life. I think this experience represents a projection of his feeling of insecurity.

In reading the history of religion and in studying hospitalized patients we often come upon descriptions of visions. In patients we ordinarily consider them to be pathological. Yet there are different degrees of pathology in visions. In schizophrenia they are considered to be serious symptoms. On the other hand, an hysterical patient may have a vision which seems closer to reality. We do not consider it as serious as in schizophrenia. There are less sophisticated people of our own day who may have visions in moments of emotional excitement, particularly in the course of a religious experience, such as during a revival meeting. In history we read of similar experiences among saints, in those waves of religious fervor which have occasionally swept through the world. It has been said that Joan of Arc must have been schizophrenic. My feeling is that she was not, but that she was a religious ecstatic. The basis of my conclusion is that a schizophrenic very rarely does anything socially useful, while Joan of Arc became a leader among her people. Ignatius Loyola, the founder of the Jesuits, also had many visions, and later became an outstanding leader in his church.

In our day, people who are patients of psychiatrists with office practices do not often have such visions. Some have fleeting visual impressions, which are valuable in the course of psychotherapy as an indication of what is going on in the upper levels of the unconscious. Later on in Jungian analysis, such impressions may become much more frequent, particularly in an introverted person who finds it easier to become aware of them.

A last source of information about the unconscious is active imagination. This is a road to the unconscious which has not been used by other psychiatrists. It is therefore a new contribution that Jung has made to psychotherapy. It does not occur in the early stages of analysis, but only after other methods have been used. Augusta Jellinek (11), a psychologist in New York who is acquainted with Jung's writings, was interested in relieving the tension which is so common in stutterers. It occurred to her that if she could get them to imagine some pleasant, agreeable scene, they might become temporarily relaxed and be able to initiate speech more easily. She first directed her subjects: "Imagine a butterfly sitting on the end of your nose," and then suggested, "Imagine the butterfly flying off." The stutterer very often imagines that the butterfly flies off to a field full of flowers and trees, perhaps with a country road winding through it, a very quiet pastoral scene. He is then able to relax and speak much more freely.

This is just the sort of thing which Jung for the last twenty or thirty years has been calling "active imagination." He begins with material derived from one of the sources which we have just mentioned. For example, he takes a patient's dream or fantasy to use consciously as a starting point. The patient purposely daydreams, as it were, in order to help himself get well or to learn about his unconscious mind. After sufficient practice, many people can carry on this activity for half an hour or more and with considerable value in their analyses. In some subjects these experiences may attain almost the clarity of visions, though always with an awareness of their lack of reality. A technique such as this must be used judiciously. It would not be a safe procedure with people already deficient in their contact with reality, such as severe neurotics or schizophrenics. It has been very useful with people who are in training for analysis, or with patients with personality problems but who still have good contact with reality.

This technique has historical analogies also. I have already mentioned Saint Ignatius Loyola. In his spiritual exercises he once developed a very similar means for encouraging spiritual meditation among his followers. His method, however, was much less spontaneous than the psychological one since he had to confine it within the framework of his strict religious doctrines.

In the writings of the Hindu yoga practitioners a very similar method for stimulating the imagination is described.

It does not take long to discover that the unconscious has a language of its own, which differs considerably from that of the average person or of the scientist. This language is a primitive one such as is seen in fairy tales, legends and mythology. It uses metaphors much more than we habitually do, and continually resorts to personification. In short, it is poetical.

As we study the material produced from different sources of information concerning the unconscious, we find that certain characteristic figures appear again and again. First, human beings, some of whom we recognize and some who are completely unknown to us, of either sex and of various ages. There are animal forms, domestic and wild, some highly evolved like monkeys and dogs, others less so, like reptiles and amphibians. There may be fantastic creatures such as are not seen on the earth but like those portrayed in ancient mythology. I recall once dreaming of ducks swimming in a pond. Suddenly, to my surprise, the ducks developed human faces which looked at me. We may dream of inanimate objects and situations: roads, mountains, lakes, oceans, automobiles, or street cars. We may dream of abstractions, including geometrical figures such as squares, circles or spirals.

Before probing down into the deeper levels of the unconscious, let us first look into the <u>personal unconscious</u>: in Jungian language called the <u>shadow</u>. If we think of the conscious as a source of light and of the persona as being erected to allow us to see into the outer world and protect ourselves from it, we can visualize the persona as casting a shadow. If we face the light, as we do except when we are asleep, or during one of the other techniques and experiences I have already described, we do not see our shadow, and prefer to be unaware of it. We associate darkness and night with ignorance and fear. The shadow originates from the repression of thoughts, impulses and feelings not acceptable to the persona. It also contains the unexpressed attitudes and functions of the personality. That is, in an extravert, the shadow contains introverted tendencies; in an introvert, it contains extraverted tendencies. Similarly with the functions: the inferior function and portions of the auxiliary functions reside in the shadow. If one is a sensation type, intuition is there. Should one be a thinking type, it is feeling that is unexpressed. These functions, because less developed and differentiated, are primitive and impulsive in their expression.

In studying the personal unconscious, we first come upon personifications of the unacceptable capacities. In dreams they are represented by persons unknown to the dreamer, and of the same sex. They are often disreputable people: tramps, criminals, prostitutes, alcoholics, and the like. In anxiety dreams they may chase or threaten the dreamer. In waking life, these figures from the negative side of the shadow are often projected upon people about us. We find them in the people of whom we are frightened, against whom we are prejudiced, whom we do not like. It is easier to project them upon people who have hooks upon which we can hang them. That is why so many people are vindictive toward those of whose behavior they do not approve: alcoholics, delinquents, criminals, and prostitutes, and explains the delight usually taken in seeing such people arrested and punished.

We may also project our shadows upon people who are not doing anything reprehensible, but are merely different. Such are members of minority groups, or citizens of another country with which our own government is on bad terms. A person who belongs to a minority group himself, may project his shadow upon one of the majority. Another common form of projection exists when a person directs his shadow toward his own child of the same sex whose behavior he does not like. That is why, even though we know better, we may lose our tempers and treat the child badly. This sort of behavior is particularly likely to be indulged in by people at home, when they are away from their persona: for example, the business man away from his office, a professional man from his practice.

Another from of projection is that of the group shadow. In most organized groups, such as exist in offices, factories, or hospitals, there are usually one or two people who provide most of the material for conversation at lunch. Such a person is different enough from the average so that the group finds him easy to criticize and dislike. No one has a good word to say for him, yet it is tacitly recognized that the group would not be the same without him.

I will not say anything more about this negative aspect of the personal unconscious, since it is the especial preserve of the psychoanalysts. They have described this part of the human psyche with great vividness. The analytical psychologist may dislike much of their technical terminology but still cannot deny that it is very picturesque and arresting. It has kept the attention of the public, including the medical profession, focused on this important part of the psyche.

The shadow has also a positive aspect. In its deeper layer it has a certain amount of illumination. This lighted portion may appear later on in analysis, after the dark side has been recognized, admitted, and accepted. At that point the guide figure will appear in unconscious productions. One of the rather disreputable people mentioned earlier will now take a more agreeable role. Often he will lead the dreamer down stairs, to a beach or riverbank, or into a building where new experiences open out. The dreamer is in this way led deeper into the unconscious, to more profound levels of understanding and potential psychological growth. The reason why this can be is because the repressed or unexpressed attitude and functions found in the unconscious are sources of energy for future growth. The ego, in its ignorance, may consider them irrelevant or useless, but if the person is going to develop a more harmonious and healthier personality, he must make use of these neglected portions of his psyche. One way in which this may be encouraged is by suggesting to a patient with recurrent anxiety dreams of being chased by some horrible figure, that in his next dream he will be able to turn and face it and see what happens. In some patients it may change into something much less dangerous, perhaps into a guide such as I have just been describing. This is a common eventuality in fairy tales, where the beast so often changes into the handsome prince. It is as though the conscious mind, through the analyst, were able to speak to the unconscious.

Much of a neurotic's psychic energy may be locked up in the shadow. But even in the case of a normal person, a great deal of psychic energy may still be unavailable to the ego. Through analysis this energy may be freed for the journey into the deeper levels of the unconscious to discover creative potentialities which could not be used previously. At this point it may be found that the person's dreams will become more productive, with more vivid imagery. Drawings and paintings may become more meaningful, and lead to deeper understanding. Intuitions may arise which enable the patient to gain better insight.

Before moving on to a more detailed description

of the collective unconscious, let me quote directly from Dr. Jung: "The collective unconscious, being an inheritance of the possibility of ideas, is not individual but generally human, generally animal even, and represents the real foundations of the individual man. It seems to consist of something of the nature of mythological themes or images. For this reason the myths of people are the real exponents of the collective unconscious . . . a kind of projection of it. The unconscious, as the totality of all archetypes, is the deposit of all human experience back to its most remote beginning. . . a living system of reactions and aptitudes determining the individual life in invisible ways."(14) It is invisible to the person concerned as well as to those who know him. The word archetype is the one which Jung most frequently uses to describe a possibility for developing images and symbols from the unconscious. Archetypes are also called primordial images or dominants of the collective unconscious. Another definition is as follows: "Archetypes are the form that the instincts have assumed. . . The unconscious is the source of the creative impulses through these archetypes." In still another place Jung says, "Archetypes are systems of preparedness that are at the same time images and emotions. They are inherited with the structure of the brain of which they are the psychic aspect."(14) They remind one very much of the Platonic ideas. Plato, however, spoke of his ideas more in terms of geometric figures than as animal figures or objects and situations. They remind one also of conceptions of the Gestalt psychologists. Those who have studied Gestalt psychology will recall that certain forms seem to be preferred by the normal human mind. If we draw, for example, a group of lines or dots arranged circularly, the naive person, filling in the gaps unconsciously, describes it as a circle. There is also an analogy with the development of the body. The zygote directly after fertilization contains within it, we do not know just how, a preparedness for the structure of the human body. Similarly, the infant mind contains the preparedness for the development of those images and their accompanying emotions which play such a great part in its psychological development in later years.

Two quotations from Sigmund Freud should remind us that he developed, although to a much lesser degree, a somewhat similar concept. He says, "In the first place it can hardly have escaped anyone that we base everything upon the assumption of a psyche of the mass in which psychic processes occur as in the psychic life of the individual. Moreover, we let the sense of guilt for a deed (the killing of the father) survive for thousands of years, remaining effective in generations which could not have known anything of this deed. We allow an emotional process such as might have arisen among generations which had escaped such treatment by the very removal of the father."(5) For example, a child who is born posthumously may have a full-fledged Oedipus complex though he never knew his father. "With out the assumption of a mass psyche, or a continuity in the emotional life of mankind which permits us to disregard the interruptions of psychic acts through the transgression of individuals, social psychology could not exist at all. If psychic processes of one generation do not continue in the next, if each had to acquire its attitude toward life afresh, there would be no progress in this field and almost no development . . . A part of the task seems to be performed by inheritance of psychic dispositions which, however, need certain incentives in the individual life in order to become effective." He does not use the word archetype, but a strong resemblance in concepts is evident. Later, Freud said in his "Moses and Monotheism,"(6): "A new complication arises, however, when we become aware that there probably exists in the mental life of the individual not only what he has experienced himself, but also what he brought with him at birth, fragments of phylogenetic origin, an archaic heritage. Then the question arises: in what does this inheritance consist, what does it contain, and what evidence of it is there? The first and most certain answer is that it consists in certain dispositions such as all living beings possess; that is to say, in the ability and tendency to follow a certain direction of development and to react in a particular way to certain excitations, impressions, and stimuli. Since experience shows that individuals differ in this respect, our archaic inheritance includes these differences; they represent what is recognized as the constitutional element in the individual." It would be difficult to be clearer in defining the collective unconscious and the nature of its archetypes. Since these have been his principal preoccupation through the last thirty years, Jung has developed these concepts much further. He has written, as it were, a geography and an anthropology of the id.

4

ARCHETYPES OF THE COLLECTIVE UNCONSCIOUS

ANALYTICAL PSYCHOLOGISTS are not above using the same sort of argument that the psychoanalysts use, that is, that our resistances to exploration of the unconscious may be due to the type of personality that we have or the kind of bringing-up that we have had. For example, it is much harder for the extravert than it is for the introvert to think of his inner psychological life in the terms Jung has described. It is also, I suspect, more difficult for the thinking type than for the intuitive type. There are cultural difficulties as well. Modern man is very proud of his achievements in the exploration of the external world and the control which he has been able to get over it through scientific and industrial methods. He is apt to look down on symbolism and ritual, such as were dominant in the middle ages in the West, or are still current in India, as mystical and obscure. Jung maintains that modern man has gone too far to the other extreme. He does not wish to minimize any of the scientific or industrial achievements nor does he recommend giving them up. He feels merely that they need to be balanced by corresponding exploration and knowledge of the inner world.

People who belong to one of the institutional religions of our day have a special problem. If they take the doctrines and rituals of their religions seriously these effectually contain certain projections from the inner world. He who goes on his own individual trip into this realm, may be faced with the necessity of changing some of his religious concepts, or, at least, of reconsidering them in a different light. That may require intellectual and spiritual activity of an unaccustomed sort.

It was said that most introverts find it easier to study this side of the mind than extraverts do. But there are other introverts who may find it expecially difficult because they are afraid of being overwhelmed by the archetypes, of being swept off their feet and perhaps pushed into mental disorder. This is what characteristically happens in schizophrenia. Introverts are especially liable to that disease, just as extraverts are more liable to manic-depressive psychosis. Consequently, a fairly strong ego structure is necessary in order to attempt to assimilate the archetypes.

All archetypal experiences share certain general characteristics. In primitive societies, the chiefs and medicine men have an aura of fear and majesty which is called "mana." When archetypes manifest themselves in our dreams or fantasies, or when they are projected into the external world, these same feelings of awe, uncanniness, and the supernatural are present. These are also the qualities which distinguish "big" or cosmic dreams from everyday ones. In addition, these archetypal presentations often have a certain fascination for us, qualities of ambiguity, intimation, and inexhaustibility of meaning, so that it is very difficult to describe all the feelings which they arouse in us or the possibilities which they may contain. Consequently, in former days when persons had dreams or visions of this type, they would seldom report them in their original form. They would feel much better after they had reconstructed them in terms of the religion or philosophy of their day. Dr. Jung once wrote a paper (8) concerning Nicholas von der Flue, a saintly man who lived in Switzerland in the fifteenth century. A record has been left of his greatest religious experience. At first very terrified, he retired into solitude to meditate about it for some time. Finally, becoming convinced his experience was a symbolic revelation of God, he was able to assimilate it. Then he was able to tell of his experience and to become a spiritual leader of his time.

We do not experience archetypes directly any more than we see atoms directly. An archetype is a theoretical construct, just as atoms and electrons are, inferred from the images and symbols of human experience. I have said before that the collective unconscious seems to be incurably personifying. Therefore, it is natural that these archetypes should usually appear in our dreams and fantasies as human beings. However, they also appear nearly as often in the form of non-human symbols. A symbol can be an object taken from everyday life such as an animal, a plant, or a geometrical figure, which is endowed with a special meaning beyond that which it ordinarily holds. It can express in itself a world of meaning which is not readily put into words.

Some of the principal archetypes of the collective unconscious can now be described. The guide function of the shadow, which I mentioned earlier, already has a certain archetypal flavor about it, although not to the extent of the others. The first figure that we come upon in dreams and fantasies or as projections into the outer world, which has the full character of an archetype, is the soul image. Jung considers this figure in two parts, one for the male sex and one for the female. To the male soul-image he gives the name anima and to the female animus. To those who remember their Latin, this may seem paradoxical. The reason for the inversion of genders is that they represent the feminine and masculine aspects of the male and female psyches respectively. The embryologists tell us that each of us has within his body some potentialities of the other sex. This conception is also held by depth psychologists, but at the psychological level rather than at the physical level alone.

The anima represents those feelings and those tendencies toward close interpersonal relationships which are often poorly developed in the masculine mind in our culture; in other words, unconscious Eros as opposed to conscious Logos development. Beyond this, she represents the creative principle in the masculine mind. It is not accidental that ancient authors thought of the muses as women. Most of the ancient artists, poets and musicians were men (with an occasional exception like Sappho) and, naturally enough, they chose feminine figures to represent the sources of their inspiration. In the dreams of individuals under analysis the anima is therefore represented by feminine figures who are usually young and attractive. In the man who is not particularly aware of his subjective life, the anima is presented as projected upon feminine figures in his environment. In his earliest years this is the mother; as he grows older, a sister (if he has one); later, a woman with whom he is in love; and still later, ideally, his wife. Poets, artists and musicians sometimes find the anima in a femme inspiratrice. Wagner, the composer, had several of them.

In the development of the male child, it is very important, if psychological growth is to progress as it should, that these transitions should take place smoothly. But they do not always go so well. The mother may be represented in dreams as a witch or other frightening female figure when she is over-protective or in some other way holds her son back from his natural development. As the psychoanalysts have pointed out, incestuous desires may arise, but Jung insists that much more than mere physical sexuality may also be implied. This subject is entered into at length in Jung's "Psychology of the Unconscious "(12).

The anima may be projected upon other figures or institutions beyond those within our immediate knowledge. In religion, legend and mythology, she has been embodied in goddesses of beauty, wisdom or love. Among Catholics, carefully avoiding, of course, all overt sexual implications, she may be projected upon the Virgin Mary. In literature, we find many such figures described. Jung is particularly fond of citing H. Rider Haggard's novel entitled "She." (9) The central figure embodies, in a remarkable way, both positive and negative aspects of the anima. The title: "She-Who-Must-Be-Obeyed," gives one the feeling of mana. H. G. Wells wrote a story called "The Sea-Lady" (23) in which a young man is carried away into the ocean by a mermaid. In the course of the normal development of the male, we commonly observe two motives: first, the escape from the anima, and, later, the return to it.

The animus, being the masculine aspect of the female, is contained in her thinking function rather than in that of feeling; in the Logos principle rather than the Eros. In our culture, men occasionally recognize a woman for her thinking ability, but only reluctantly and with some feelings of apprehensiveness. This helps to explain why some women must be so assertive when they are exercising the thinking function, even when they are doing a very good job of it. In the dream, the animus is represented by masculine figures, often handsome, heroic strangers of a somewhat mysterious aspect. The animus is projected in a manner similar to that of the anima first upon the father, then successively upon a brother, lover, husband, or even upon a son if the woman happens to have married a man who does not adequately represent her animus. A woman may also project her animus upon religious leaders, even upon the figure of Jesus himself. In our culture the animus has only been recently freed from patriarchal bondage. There was a time when women were not supposed to find out that they had an animus at all. Some militant women of the last few generations, such as the "Suffragettes" and founders of women's colleges, were first able to express the animus in Western Europe and America. Mrs. Jung, in her excellent essay on the problem of the animus, points out that the introduction of contraception has given many women time and energy, formerly occupied in raising innumerable children, for realizing their creative ambitions. This process of freeing the animus is still going on. Now it is much easier for us to recognize that women may become intellectual leaders and creative in fields which had formerly been reserved for men. A woman can more readily be a leader and still remain feminine.

In the male, the archetype of the hero often appears in the form of a companion to the anima, as an unknown man who is not disreputable like the shadow, but has all the positive qualities we associate with the highest type of youthful male. In the dream he may be represented as a knight who kills either a human antagonist or a horrifying mythological creature. He thus symbolizes the conquest of the negative figures in the unconscious, whether shadow figures or negative aspects of the anima. In the female, this figure is apt to coalesce with the animus so that the woman may dream of an athlete, political leader or spiritual hero who combines both archetypes. In antiquity, this archetype was very frequently projected into legendary heroes, among them Gilgamesh in Babylonian times, Samson in the Old Testament, Hercules among the Greeks, and Siegfried in German legend. Religious founders and saints embodied this same archetype in the minds of their devout followers, just as did in Medieval days the chivalric knights, Gawain, Galahad, Roland and others. In modern times, because the ability to compose legends has been nearly lost, we are more apt to make heroes of living military and political leaders. If these men are beneficent, they represent the positive aspect of the hero. Unfortunately the hero has his negative aspect as well, which may be embodied in demonic leaders like Adolf Hitler. The hero figure may thus become dangerous to civilization. When this happens in the future, I hope we will be more aware of what is going on than we have been in the past, so that we will nip such men in the bud.

As these first archetypes are near the surface of the collective unconscious they often are encountered in the early stages of analysis. For the same reason they also occur spontaneously in the fantasies and projections of normal people. Other archetypes occur only in the later stages of analysis, except perhaps in a few people who are more sensitive than most of us to emanations from the collective unconscious. They often appear as well in the delusions of schizophrenics. First, there is the figure of the old wise man, usually white-haired and venerable, who speaks with great authority, in a traditional and proverbial way. Jung speaks of "the archetypal old man, who, beyond good and evil, is the superior master and teacher, a pointer of the way, the preexistent meaning concealed in chaotic life, the father of the soul, the enlightener, the archetype of meaning." (16) This archetype is sometimes projected upon an old professor, greatly venerated in a University. The Chinese have enshrined it in the figures of Confucius and Lao Tze. In our civilization, where youth is venerated and the old are so often looked down upon or neglected, we do not have much opportunity to project this archetype. It therefore lives only in the unconscious.

Jung next describes the archetypes of transformation. During analysis or in the process of the natural growth of the individual, they may appear in the form of situations, journeys, animals or plants which symbolize change or transformation. In our dreams, for example, we may see ourselves going down long flights of stairs, entering caves, tunnels, or deep forests, or traveling along winding roads. We may be led along these paths and into these situations by animal figures or we may find remarkable trees and flowers on our way. Animals may grow larger before our eyes or transform themselves into other figures. These all symbolize psychological growth, the journey into the unconscious, and all its accompanying dangers. The archetypes of transformation may also appear in the form of initiation ceremonies. In modern civilized life we see them in a reduced form in college fraternities, and in a more developed form among the Masons, Knights of Columbus, and other fraternal organizations. In primitive cultures initiation has a much larger place than in ours. Every male has to undergo the ceremony. As an example of how these archetypal situations may appear in the dream life of a modern man I would like to quote a dream reported to a psychotherapist. "I dreamed I was a Negro, living in an African village. I was happy and contented and seemed to enjoy life and all it had. Then I got a message from the king, a witch doctor, saying that he wanted to talk to me. I went to visit him in a stone building, more out of curiosity than anything else, wondering why he wanted to see me. I went down a long hallway and came to a small ante-chamber. There, I saw a basrelief or statue and it was on the right side of the wall from which issued a voice. I was more curious than frightened and looked at the statue and realized it was just a trick to impress me. So later, I heard a voice and the door opened and I entered a room where the witch priest was. He spoke to me and called me "Son" and told me why he wanted to see me. He was a tall, strong man and except for his grizzled grey hair, showed little sign of age. He told me he was getting old and that custom had it that he could choose his successor and teach him and give him the powers he had, to be used by his successor after he passed on. He explained that he knew the secrets and rites, and as a witch-priest he would, if I desired and wanted his position, initiate me as his disciple to succeed him when he passed on. He explained the initiation ceremonies and I was initiated." Many of the archetypes which I have been describing are clearly represented in this dream.

Animals in various habitats and at various levels of evolutionary development may symbolize different things. Mammals and birds represent higher instinctive tendencies. Birds may, for example, represent potential thoughts or spiritual aspirations since our thoughts are often impractically far above the ground. Amphibians may represent tendencies which bridge the gap between the conscious world, the earth, and the unconscious world, the water. All cold-blooded animals, whether amphibians or reptiles, often represent the more primitive instincts which are harder for us to understand because they come from the deeper levels of the unconscious.

Lastly, we come to the Self. This is a difficult archetype both to understand and to explain. The Self in Jung's psychology is contrasted with the smaller "self" that is the ego, or with that part of the ego which we have called the persona. It is the principle of harmony, balance and integration in the human mind. It is the archetype which Jung was last to discover perhaps because it is at the greatest depth and the most abstract. It is the psychological counterpart to the principle of homeostasis, a word we use to describe the manner in which the human body, impinged upon from all sides by changes in the environment which would tend to upset its equilibrium, manages to maintain a fairly constant balance. Though we may from day to day or even from one hour to the next, experience violent changes in external temperature, eat foods of varying chemical composition, engage in strenuous physical activity or remain at rest, there are physiological mechanisms which successfully maintain, or at least restore, a relatively invariable composition of the blood, a fairly steady internal temperature and blood pressure. Just as we have homeostasis in our physiological process, so we have a balancing, harmonizing principle in the psyche.

If a person becomes psychotic and then recovers, his personality returns to its same integrity. It may be supposed that the Self retained this capacity for integrity during the patient's illness. It is a sort of Jungian super-ego, but, it is easy to see, of a very different quality from Freud's. It is not learned from the outside, from parents and teachers, but is within the human mind all the while. It is true that much we learn from our parents and teachers may be of a harmonizing nature, particularly if it is well learned and integrated with our other experiences. But even if we disregard as far as possible what we learned from our elders, we can still discover within us an even deeper conscience.

In dreams the Self may be represented by a person, such as a King or Emperor. More commonly, in these republican times, it is represented in the form of an astronomical body such as the sun or a star, by a geometrical figure such as a circle, square, wheel, or by a clock, flower, or perhaps an egg. The egg is a particularly meaningful symbol because it condenses so neatly potentiality for both growth and rebirth.

Searching for adequate symbolic representation of the Self, Jung discovered one in the rituals of the Buddhists of Tibet. In the course of their meditations the Tibetan monks use paintings or rugs, decorated with symbolic patterns and designs called mandalas. These are valuable aids in securing psychological and spiritual harmony. In the Christian faith the Cross is such a symbol. It is not so strictly balanced geometrically, the lower arm being longer than the other three. Since that arm connects it with the earth the alteration is a wise one because it reminds us that in our spiritual Odyssey we should be sure not to take our feet from the ground. The archetype of the Self is projected also into divine figures embodying perfection, whether incarnated upon the earth, or gods and goddesses themselves. We Western Europeans are accustomed to project the Self upon the masculine figure of the Judaeo-Christian God, but in other civilizations femine figures have contained it just as successfully.

To clarify these concepts, I would like to introduce a diagram of my own invention. (Figure 2). Above I have drawn two arrows representing the conflict of the opposites. They appear to be going in exactly opposite directions, and may represent either extraversion and introversion, or egoism and altruism. If extended indefinitely, they will never meet. We have learned recently from physics that space is curved. Let us suppose that we are dealing with an analogous phenomenon in psychology and confidently extend our arrows till they do meet. At the top of the diagram we have the ego, the arena for the conflict of the opposites. Going outward we first come to the family to which the ego must first

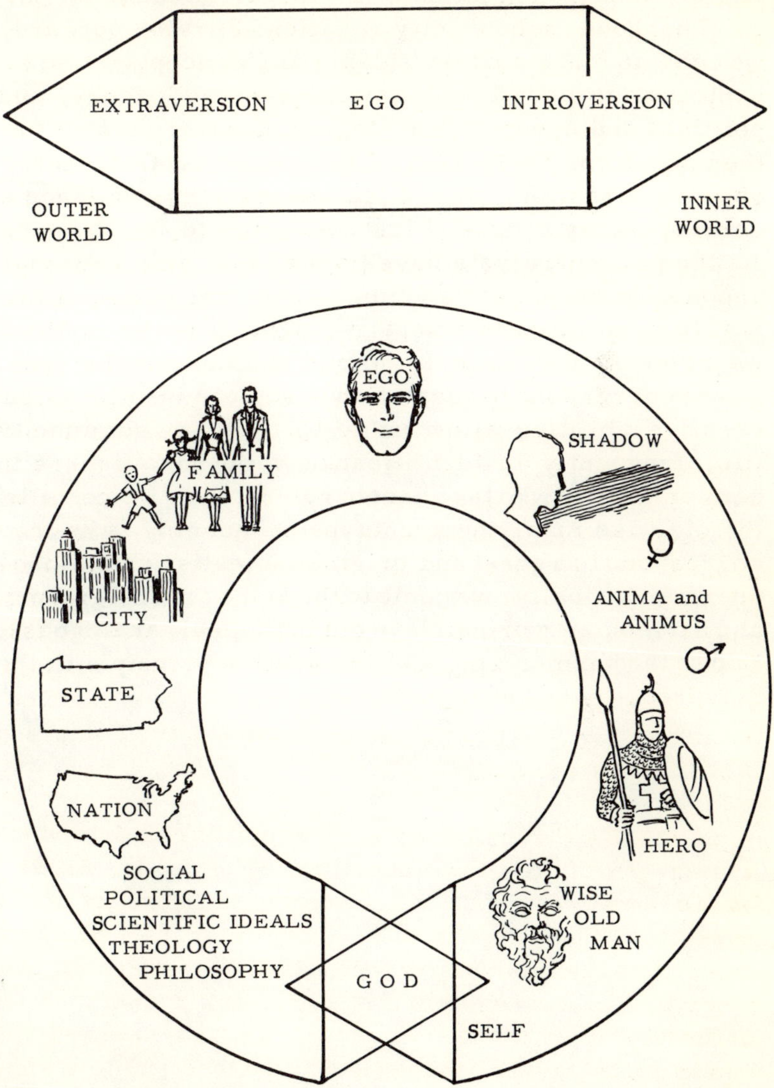

Figure 2. The uniting of the opposites through the archetypes.

adjust itself, then later to the larger community: the neighborhood, school, city or nation. Further outward, we come to more abstract ideals and concepts, represented in our modern world by science, philosophy, and political and economic ideologies. Continuing still further we come to the idea of the universal God. In the opposite direction, toward the unconscious, we trace a corresponding course. First, we come to the shadow. As the psychoanalysts have pointed out, this personal unconscious represents primarily the reflection of the family most often in a negative light. If we go further, we come to the anima, animus and hero archetypes. These correspond to adaptation to society insofar as our creative abilities allow us to be useful in community life, frequently in identification with those figures in our community who take heroic roles. Then we come to the old wise man, the archetype of meaning, who may correspond to a great and original scientist or philosopher. And, finally, we come to the Self, the integrating, and harmonizing principle in the individual, analogous to God as the harmonizing and integrating principle in the universe.

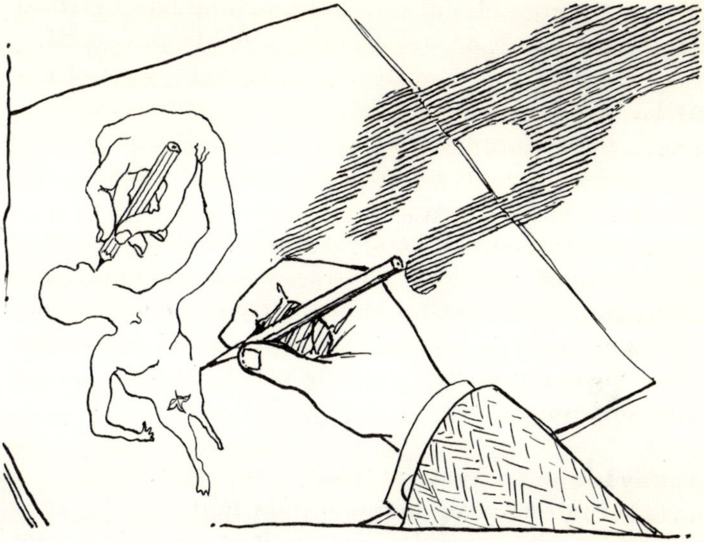

5

THE TECHNIQUE OF ANALYSIS

IN SOME RESPECTS, the techniques of Jungian and Freudian analysis are similar. There is one patient and one analyst. The therapist is expected to be analyzed before he takes up his practice. Many terms are used in common, such as the unconscious, identification, projection, transference and countertransference. But still, there are a good many differences.

In the beginning of the analysis, it is customary among analytical psychologists, as well as among many psychoanalysts, to attempt to determine in advance the depth of treatment indicated. The nature of the problem

*The figure above is adapted from one drawn by a patient described in H. G. Baynes, Mythology of the Soul, p. 525 (1).

is an important consideration. If the patient has definite symptoms for which he asks relief, if his personality structure seems to be quite highly developed and his adaptation fairly good, then all that may be necessary is to clear up the symptoms. If there seems to be a fairly deep-seated character disorder, or if the person complains less of specific symptoms, than of general feelings of uncertainty about the meaning of his life, despite a good external adjustment, then a deep analysis may be indicated. However, one must be cautious, because unless a person has a reasonably strong ego, he may not be able to withstand the uncovering of the deeper levels of his unconscious.

It is easy for an analyst, at least an inexperienced one, to be so fascinated by the unconscious that he may forget how important the ego is, or take it for granted. But it is the ego which has to do much of the work. If its most highly developed attitude and function are not enlisted as allies, then the investigation of the unconscious cannot go forward. An analysis is a cooperative adventure, not only between the ego and the analyst, but also between the ego and the unconscious. It is as though the ego were struggling with two impersonal worlds–the world outside the external environment, and the equally impersonal world within–the collective unconscious. We think of the external world as impersonal because it happens to us. Similarly, events from the depths of the unconscious just happen. This is most obvious in connection with one's dreams. We go to sleep and dream whatever comes along. In trying to understand this and other material from the inner world, the ego must accept its responsibility and do its share of the work.

The management of a Jungian analysis should be distinguished by its flexibility. The details of the technique must be adapted to the individual patient's needs and personality. In most cases the patient and the analyst sit facing each other. Yet there is no reason why the patient cannot turn toward the window, or walk up and down, or why he and the analyst cannot walk outdoors if the sun is shining in the garden. Frequency of interviews can be variable. In the beginning of analysis, when the analyst and the patient are getting acquainted, and when there may be a good deal of anxiety, rather frequent interviews are indicated, perhaps three or four each week. As the analysis gets beyond this phase, two sessions a week are usually enough. It is possible, too, to have more than one analyst. The same person may go for a while to a male analyst and then to a female one—or the other way around. This can be valuable because analysts have different personalities, and one may draw out things the other does not. It is essential that the two analysts get together now and then and discuss the case. The Jungian seems to rely more upon vacations than does the average Freudian analyst. The former feels that it is not only a matter of convenience for the analyst but also useful for the patient to be "allowed out to grass" every few months so that he can consolidate the progress he has made and work matters out on his own. If irregularity of treatment is unavoidable because the patient or the analyst has to be away, it is therefore not considered a calamity.

Jung considers the transference a matter of very great importance. In fact, he has written a book (17) dealing solely with this subject. Unfortunately, it has not yet been translated into English, but I will give you a quotation from it to illustrate his viewpoint in his early years. "What high significance Freud places on the transference phenomena was first made clear to me at the time of our first personal meeting in 1907. After an interview lasting many hours, a pause came. Suddenly he asked me, without preparation, 'and what do you think of the transference? I answered, from my deepest conviction that it is the Alpha and the Omega of the analytic method.

Thereupon, he said, 'Then you have understood that which is most important.'" He goes on to say: "The great significance of the transference has given much opportunity for error." Since 1907 Jung has modified his early conviction of the extreme indispensibility of the transference. In Jungian analysis it is not encouraged and cultivated to the extent that it is by Freudian analysts. It is felt that a relationship of confidence between the analyst and analysand is essential, but projection of his neurotic trends upon the analyst is discouraged. If such a relationship does develop (and it is recognized that this may be unavoidable in many cases) then it needs to be handled with care and skill. Besides projection from the personal unconscious, which psychoanalysts have described in detail, Jung emphasizes the projection of the archetypes as well. Early in his analytical career, Jung noticed in one case that the patient seemed to be projecting much more than the father image upon him. She seemed to expect Jung to be a magician as well, and ultimately even a divine figure. To illustrate that this sort of thing may happen here as well, let me describe a dream an American patient had concerning his physician. This is how the patient related it: The doctor and he were in the doctor's office, when suddenly a verv tiny man in a black cape and hat opened the door and came into the office. The patient jumped up, pushed the chair back, and said to the little man "Even in this office you come to bother me, but there is even a greater sorcerer than you here." The doctor had grown very tall, and was also dressed in a black cape. The patient then said to the little man, "He'll get rid of you." He evidently hoped that the shadow figure would be exorcised by the doctor's sorcery.

Apatient may think of a male analyst as both a father and a mother figure, at once, for the therapist's anima is in the situation as well as his ego. When the analyst is a woman the situation is reversed. The physician must also consider his own collective unconscious. He may identify with his own hero or divinity archetype and suffer from an inflation which will interfere with his ability as an analyst.

The Jungian analyst relies strongly upon the interpretation of dreams. He also relies very greatly upon spontaneous paintings and drawings, as the following passage from "The Integration of the Personality" (16) shows: "Because pictorial expression fixes certain unconscious contents and draws others around it, the patient can work magic by this means, but only upon himself. Instead of being merely in a subjective state, he is confronted with objective form that reflects the psychoolgical situation." Many times a patient will object, when asked to draw or paint, that he cannot do it, that he had no skill or training in art. It is always wise for the analyst to encourage him to try anyhow by saying that he is not an art critic and that he is only interested in productions from the unconscious. The diffidence may be a species of resistance. In this connection, referring to a female patient, Jung wrote: "She could hardly paint at all so I advised her simply to portray the human figure in the form of a hieroglyph or sketch, but to execute everything else as carefully as possible." He goes on to say: "Like a child or primitive man, the unconscious loves to see its contents represented in the brightest colors. That exercises upon it a magical attraction." Consequently, paintings are better than drawings, water colors, oils, and finger paints are preferable to pencil. "Drawing or painting is right only if done upon inner motivation. The pictures ought to make themselves." The patient should be encouraged to draw whatever comes into his head and allow the sequence of pictures to develop naturally. Often a patient complains that he cannot think of anything to draw. He can be advised to make wavy lines or geometrical figures and continue with whatever they spontaneously suggest. (See also (1).

Analytical psychologists consider it essential to record dreams and fantasies carefully. At first it is wise for the patient or student to write out every dream, whether it seems significant or not. This is not only because the patient is unable to tell what may or may not be significant, but also because it gives practice in observing dreams, and so trains the introverted sensation function. Explanatory notes are made where needed—that is, concerning incidents or persons which the analyst would not otherwise know about. Then context material is recorded, that is, relevant objective data suggested by the persons and incidents in the dream. As the analysis progresses, the patient may attempt his own interpretations. Certain themes appear as a dream series goes on. One may dream about similar subjects on successive nights, but more commonly several themes interweave as in a symphony. It is therefore not only desirable to interpret each dream singly, but also a whole series. A dream which by itself seemed to mean very little may be expanded in later ones. I recall such a series which I had myself, all having to do with water. In the first dream someone told me that there was a flood, but I did not see any water. In the next one I was down on the shore of a river overflowing its banks. I just watched it and no more. A few nights later, I picked up my courage, waded in the water and swam downstream. Coming to a bridge which was so nearly covered that to get under the arch I would have had to dive, I turned around and swam back. In the following dream the flood was apparently over, and the arches of the bridge were above me so that I could wade into the shallows toward the deeper water on the other side.

The mood or atmosphere of a dream should always be considered. When the analysis is not going well, or external events are menacing, dreams may have a gloomy, unpleasant atmosphere of darkness, cloudiness, or rain. If, however, progress is being made, a cheerful sunny atmosphere will be present.

Dreams of any length have a dramatic structure. First, one finds a certain situation, indoors, outdoors, on a plain, among mountains, or by a river. Characters appear on the scene. Almost always the dreamer himself is among them. Then comes the exposition, in which the characters by their actions or conversation set the atmosphere of the play. As the dream goes on, development occurs, gradually rising to a crisis or culmination. In anxiety dreams the dream ends here and the dreamer wakes up. Such a dream usually refers to a crisis in his present life to which he needs to attend. Most dreams go on to a lysis or solution through which they are brought to a fitting close. Many brief dreams do not have all these characteristics. Only the crisis or the solution without the exposition and development are recalled.

There is one point which distinguishes Jung's approach to dreams very definitely from Freud's. Jung insists that dreams always tell the truth. The manifest content is therefore emphasized. It is the ego which obscures the meaning of the dream. The unconscious has no need to do so because it is accountable only to itself. However, some distortion may occur between the time the patient has the dream and the time that he recounts it. If the analyst does not understand what the dream is about, it is not necessarily because the patient is distorting it, but rather because the analyst has not reached that stage of perfection where he can interpret everything. Jung points out that in the very early part of an analysis, dreams may seem quite clear. Many patients have an initial dream which seems to summarize succinctly the whole of his neurosis or his character problem. Later, as the analysis brings things up from deeper levels, the dreams tend to become more obscure. Jung counsels modesty; as far as the analyst is concerned, it is much better for him to admit to the patient that he does not understand everything than to assume a non-existent omniscience.

Because each dream is unique, a problem in itself, it must be approached with a completely open mind. Although characteristic plots and symbols frequently recur, dreams are continually surprising in their novelty. One can never presume, just because a dream is similar to one that another patient has had, that it means the same. It must be interpreted in view of what one knows about preceding dreams and about the life of the patient under treatment.

Other dynamisms which Jung discusses are similar to those Freud describes. Contamination is present when one figure merges more or less with another. If a male patient dreams of a hermaphrodite, it may mean that the shadow is contaminated by the anima. Where different traits of one person appear in several dream characters, it means that multiplication has taken place. In accordance with the primitive nature of dream-thinking, abstractions are concretized as people or symbols. As far as material from the collective unconscious is concerned, archaization takes place. The collective images are presented in the form of figures resembling those of antique or primitive mythology and legend. As Alfred Storch pointed out years ago, this process is common in the formation of the delusions of schizophrenics (22), and is seen in dreams of normal and neurotic people as well.

When the dreams have been assessed in the manner that I have described, then we are ready to amplify the various figures and symbols individually. First, we consider whether they are objective or subjective. If they are people to whom one has close emotional relationships, then their objective nature is evident. That does not mean, however, that only an objective meaning is implied since subjective tendencies may be present also insofar as the individuals in question are bearers of projections from the unconscious. If the figures are unknown to the dreamer, or if in addition they have symbolic and archaic implications, then only a subjective meaning can be inferred.

Sexual dreams may offer particular problems. If the person in the sexual relationship is the patient's wife, husband, or lover, and sexual excitement is felt, then a sexual meaning is unmistakably intended. If the sexual dream does not involve anyone with whom one is acquainted or if the ego shows no evidence of sexual excitement, then an objective sexual reference is not necessarily meant. The rest of the initiation dream from the last talk can serve as an illustration. The old Negro medicine man who was initiating the dreamer performed fellatio upon him and bit off the tip of his penis, as the culmination of the ceremony. The patient interpreted this as evidence of unconscious homosexuality or of a castration complex. These are logical conclusions, but not the whole story. The patient felt no sexual excitement in the dream, and the sexual act appeared undisguised. It is well known that according to Freudian theory sexual contents are supposed to be hidden by symbols or signs. Here, since they were not hidden, the phallus may itself be a symbol. As we learn from comparative religion, the phallus symbolizes male creativity and power. Such an interpretation is helpful in understanding this dream at a deeper level.

Dreams have various functions, depending considerably upon the conscious situation of the dreamer. If the patient is over-emphasizing some portion of the ego or persona, then the dream will be <u>compensatory</u> and call attention to the repressed or unexpressed side of the psyche. A <u>prospective</u> function may be indicated, pointing to some future possibility of personality development and growth. If the patient has plunged deeply into discouragement, this information may be very uplifting. When the ego is evaluating itself too highly, or trying to assume responsibilities which are too much for its capacity, then the dreamer may be presented in some ridiculous or devaluating role.

These functions which I have just described apply largely to the everyday dreams concerned with the personal unconscious or the upper layer of the collective unconscious. But when so-called "big," cosmic, or collective dreams occur, different handling is necessary. The patient is able to give little or no context material. The figures which appear are more abstract and formal and therefore have to be interpreted in more general terms. To understand them the analyst must have a wide and profound knowledge of fairy tales, myths, legends and comparative religion. These materials from man's historical past and from primitive tribes are sources for the amplification of collective dreams.

As psychotherapy goes on, a great many interpretations may occur to the analyst. If he is inexperienced, he may feel that he has to divulge all of them to the patient as soon as he thinks of them. Because of his own feelings of insecurity, he may wish to impress his patient and so build up his own ego. The skilled analyst, on the other hand, interprets to the patient only as much as is necessary at the point reached in the analysis. This may depend upon what the patient's ego is able to bear without undue anxiety. If too much is interpreted too early, the patient may become frightened and leave analysis, or a negative transference may develop. It is important, therefore, that interpretations be put forward in the form of suggestions rather than in a dogmatic way, and that the assent of the patient be gained as one goes along. Several possible interpretations may occur to the analyst, and each of them presented to see which one "clicks," or strikes home to the patient. If the analyst has not been influencing strongly a suggestible patient, this will most likely be the best one.

It is important to keep in mind just what the goals of analysis are: relief of symptoms, or the removal of inhibiting obstructions to personality growth. When these barriers are relieved or partially removed, the patient may be able to carry on alone after analysis is ended.

Jung emphasizes that synthesis is just as essential as analysis. In the early stages, only analysis may be going on, but in a short time synthesis must begin. As the treatment progresses, conflicts of pairs of opposites will appear. In the beginning the patient may be aware of only one of a pair, but later the other will show itself. At that point, the patient's anxiety may be increased because he is for the first time clearly aware of the tension between them. In order to reconcile them, some mediation must take place. To describe the process, Jung uses the concept of the transcendent function, operating through a reconciling symbol. The latter is also called the uniting, or integrating symbol. It is by means of it that synthesis takes place. An example is a type of conflict not uncommonly seen in adolescence or early adulthood. In a young man or woman with a moral and religious upbringing, there may be severe conflict between high moral principle and strong sexual drives. The marriage ceremony is a step toward integration through the means of their legal acceptance and religious symbolization. A satisfactory marriage becomes a goal toward whose achievement the analyst can work.

Jung noticed long ago that many of his patients seemed to continue to develop and get further relief of symptoms after they left analysis. It is possible also for a patient to return to analysis when he meets a new crisis or begins a new period of development in his life. He was originally helped during the period of early adulthood with a problem arising from marriage. Later, in the involutional period, he may have to come back for further aid because he had reached another stage of psychological development. At that time it may be observed that the second analytic course does not begin where the other left off, but that there has been considerable change and growth in the meanwhile. The process of individuation is a dynamic one, going on continually both within analysis and outside of it.

It is important to recognize that there is a close analogy between the therapeutic process in a patient with neurotic or psychotic symptoms and the development of normal personality. The psychiatrist, in treating his patient, thinks mainly in terms of bringing him from an abnormal state up to the average level. The analytical student, or the normal person seeking more harmonious growth of his personality, is thinking in terms of developing from the average or conventional level to a still higher one. In looking for means to help his patients, Jung has drawn upon knowledge derived from both normal people and comparative religion. The same methods which have helped patients are useful in developing higher levels of personality in people who are not sick. Individuation, whether in pathological individuals or in normal ones, is all one process.

6

APPLICATIONS IN PSYCHOTHERAPY.

ACCORDING TO JUNGIAN THEORY, as I see it, the reasons people get psychiatric illness can be placed under at least four headings. First is an unresolved fixation of the anima or the animus. Second is the lopsided development of an attitude or function in the course of the early years when the persona is being formed. Third is a presumable constitutional sensitivity to material from the collective unconscious so that it threatens the conscious more easily, and the personality has to erect unusually strong barriers against it. Fourth is a lack of expression of strong creative impulses. If one has not had the opportunity to express these creative impulses, because he was brought up in an environment where they were either not encouraged or were actively discouraged, then symptoms will arise. The collective unconscious contains not only material potentially pathological, but also creative potentialities which may be of therapeutic value for those who are in need of therapeutic help.

Since Jung seldom discusses case histories in terms of formal psychiatric classifications, I wish to make it clear that I am responsible for most of what follows. Let me first take up those conditions which are apt to occur in the first half of life. The first stage in normal development is attachment to the mother or father. The son's anima is projected upon the mother, and the daughter's animus is projected upon the father. Pathology consists in fixation of these projections beyond the usual age. At the next stage, the attachment may become fixed upon a brother or sister or some other male or female relative who has lived in the home.

At the unconscious level, two developments may take place. With the beginning of sexual interests and particularly if the child is very closely attached to the mother or the father, there may very well be incest phantasies. Or, more commonly, if a struggle is taking place to break away from the parents, then a negative figure will arise, initiating mixed feelings of love and hate. The mother may be portrayed in dream and phantasy as a witch, an image often referred to by Jung as that of the devouring mother. I have never heard the phrase "devouring father," but I see no reason why there should not be one.

At the conscious level there are several possible pathological developments. One is some type of psychoneurosis. Another is a condition of "sexualized spirituality," in which the person may exaggerate his interest in religion in order to escape the unrecognized conflict. This shows itself in continual preoccupation with religion, or in an obsessive-complusive neurosis with religious components. Another possibility is homosexuality. In the male, this may take the form of anima possession. Instead of projecting the anima, he identifies himself with it and acts as though he were a woman–but a mere caricature of the normal woman because he is expressing it in an unconscious undifferentiated way. Conversely, the woman who is homosexually inclined is said to have animus possession. Another form that repressed homosexuality may take is exaggerated masculinity. It may also show itself in homosexual panic or homosexual obsessions. I recall a patient of mine, for example, who felt compelled to stare at the genital region of men who were walking by. It also may show itself in homosexual acts occuring during pathological intoxication with alcohol. Many chronic alcoholics have attacks of hallucinations, hearing voices accusing them most commonly of homosexual practices, less commonly of incest and other perverse practices or threatening them with dismemberment. It is notorious that alcoholics usually have a very strong barrier between the conscious and the unconscious, so that it is very difficult to help them by psychotherapy. In the course of their hallucinations, the personal unconscious shows itself in its true colors.

One might wonder where the dismemberment fantasies come from since they do not seem to fit in with the psychoanalytic theory that repressed homosexuality is the principal trigger for alcoholism. I might make this a little clearer by citing the dream of another patient. This young man had considerable conflict over homosexuality. His married brother, a butcher, was unquestionably masculine, This is the dream: "I was out with my brother and a (male) friend of mine. Instead of butchering a hog, as my brother would, he was butchering a man. The man begged to be killed. My brother put his knife in his chest, but he did not die, so my friend turned the man over on his stomach and stabbed him in the back. He did not die right then but finally did. Then they cut his body up in pieces and just threw them about. I had to turn my back. It was the most horrible dream I have ever had. I could hardly eat the next morning." The first association to the dream was that this brother was the patient's favorite. "I admire him. He is such a good citizen and character. "One possible interpretation is that the man who is being killed is the patient's shadow, and therefore embodies his homosexual tendencies. His brother represents his persona ideal, the man that he would like to be. His unacceptable shadow is being destroyed and dismembered by the brother and the heterosexual friend. The dream shows the patient can neither accept nor repress his shadow. It may have a malignant prognostic import, because dismemberment can imply schizophrenia, in which the Self may be destroyed and reconstruction of the personality will, therefore, be impossible. It may indicate the possibility of an acute schizophrenic upset, with later remodeling of the personality. Some schizophrenics are better after an attack than before it. On the other hand, if the patient is able to accept treatment, the dream may have a good prognostic import. It may imply that a new personality is going to be born. The use of mythological material helps to understand how this interpretation is tenable. Dionysius, one of the Greek gods, was torn apart by the Titans in the course of their battle with Zeus. The parts of his body were rescued by Zeus, who ate the heart. Whereupon Dionysius was reborn through Zeus' body. Dismemberment may point toward eventual rebirth; that is, the old has to be destroyed before the new can come.

The interpretation concerning the shadow could be explained to the patient if he seemed in a position to understand it; that concerning dismemberment would be deferred to a later period of treatment. If the prognostic import is good, the Self may appear in a later dream as a protector against dismemberment.

Marital problems occur in early adulthood and frequently reach a crisis around the age of thirty-five. (14).

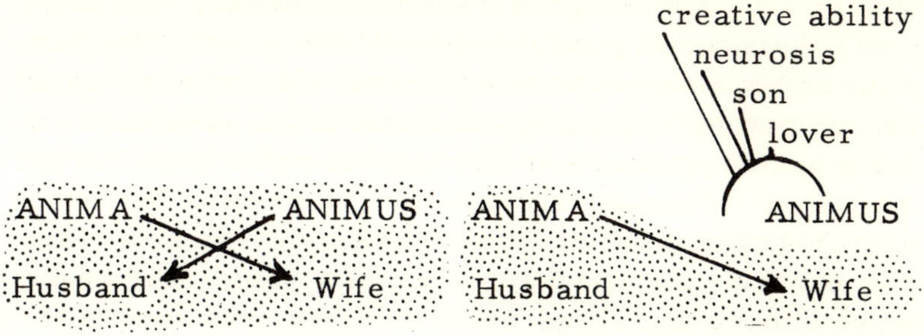

(a) Ideal situation: both satisfied.

(b) Husband satisfied; wife dissatisfied because her animus is left out of the marital relationship.

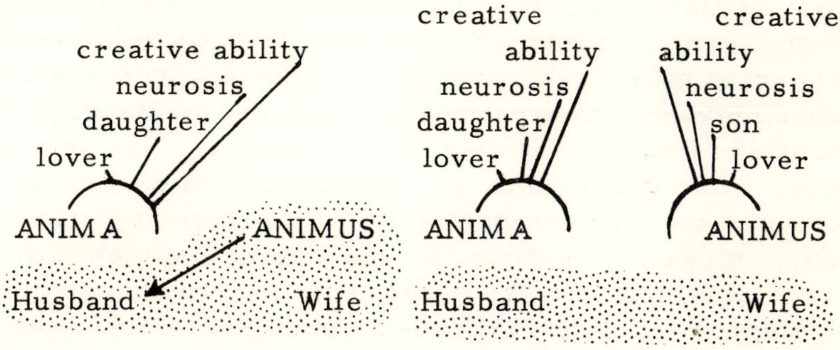

(c) Wife satisfied; husband dissatisfied because his anima is left out of the marital relationship.

(d) Both dissatisfied; both anima and animus seek satisfaction outside of the marital relationship.

Figure 3. Variations in emotional relations between husband and wife.

I have drawn some diagrams to illustrate some of the possible relationships between the husband and wife. (See Figure 3). Figure 3a represents the ideal situation, a rare condition in the later years of marriage simply because no human being is so perfect as to contain all of the partner's anima or animus. Therefore, one or the other will often be dissatisfied because the marriage partner is not an outlet for all of his or her unconscious energy. A development will then take place such as indicated in the other diagrams. In Figure 3b we suppose that the husband's anima remains absorbed in the wife, so that he continues to believe that his marriage is a happy and ideal one. Jung speaks of him, therefore, as the contained individual, and of his wife as the container. Her animus is not completely occupied in the husband. If she is sophisticated and amoral, she may find herself a lover and be satisfied with him indefinitely, or at least until she feels she needs another. If she is a woman of high moral standards, or is too repressed to take a lover she may express her animus in one of various ways. Should she have a son whom she thinks she can bring up to suit her ideal better than her husband does, she may project her animus upon him. Hence originates a great deal of maternal over-protection. "Sexualized spirituality" may show itself too. She may become attached to her clergyman, or to the leader of a cult, and think she is being very religious. Until this point everything goes on at the conscious level, as far as activity is concerned, although the motives may remain completely unconscious. At the level of the personal unconscious, however, a neurosis may develop. Passing to the next diagram, Figure 3c, the opposite situation is portrayed: the husband is the container and the wife the contained. His anima goes wandering off searching for someone to project upon. The last diagram, Figure 3d, illustrates the situation when both are dissatisfied.

Other factors are not represented in the diagrams,

for example, the different attitudes toward the sexual relationship which prevail in the average man or woman in our society. To the man, the marital relationship is apt to be secondary to his career and role outside the home. For the woman, the marital relationship should be, at least in the first half of life, her most important concern. To the husband, the sexual relationship may be an enjoyable one which helps to cement the marriage together, but it is still fundamentally physical. To the wife, however, the physical relationship is only part of the wider psychological one; women, consequently, are much more subject to frigidity or other sexual difficulties, than men are to impotence in marriage. If the marriage is not going well for her, the sexual relationship is apt to be secondarily disturbed. If the marriage otherwise is not satisfactory to the man, he may still have a relatively good sexual relationship since he is able to satisfy his ego to a large extent in his career.

With surprising frequency people of opposite types marry each other. An extravert may marry an introvert. A man with a highly differentiated thinking or sensation function often marries a woman whose feeling or intuition function is more differentiated. Such differences lead to continual misunderstanding. The husband says that his wife is illogical and emotional. If she tries to assert her rights in the home and her desires to be an individual, she will seem aggressive to him. The wife, on the other hand, continually complains that the husband is undemonstrative and inconsiderate and that he is repressing her need for self-expression. Of the patients who have come to me with marital problems, it is remarkable what a large proportion of them fit into this pattern. Very frequently they are between the ages of thirty-five and forty. The husband is usually unwilling to admit his marriage is not going well; he has outlets in his career, or can more easily have an extra-marital affair than his wife. So she more commonly comes to the psychiatrist than he.

If she is able to work it out in activity, however, she will never come to a psychiatrist. Should the mother project upon the son, or the husband upon the daughter, a neurosis-producing situation may develop, with the possibility of eventual homosexuality or neurosis in the child. We then see mother or father attachment of the kind mentioned above. Another way out is a therapeutic one which brings the husband and wife together through creative activity. If the couple have a genuine desire to make a successful marriage, and enough anima and animus attachment remains, the mere understanding of the situation in the terms I have described may help matters a great deal. But particularly in women the need for expression through creative activity may be very important. If the husband does not feel his work to be creative he will need to change his attitude toward it, find new potentialities in it, or develop absorbing outside interests so that his anima is taken up in creative activity and not in the ceaseless search for another woman. If his creative interests tend unconsciously toward artistic work, his ego may conceive it to be beneath his masculinity. The psychiatrist's role will then be to help him revise this erroneous attitude. The wife is apt to run up against opposition toward her creative aims, not only from her own preconceptions, but also from her husband's. If the husband is old-fashioned, believing the woman's place is in the home, he will not want her to be creative except through her children and in her kitchen. If she excels, he may fear that she will put him in the shade. Many women feel the need for activities outside their homes at thirty-five or forty, when their children are old enough to be going to school and are not taking up so much of their time. Since women are more commonly of the feeling type, they may go about expressing themselves in work involving human relationships, for example, in a social agency or in local politics. They may wish more individual recognition and try to make a reputation in artistic activities. Through creative accomplishments the personalities of the husband and the wife will attain much greater fulfillment and a much more harmonious relationship between them will develop than through repression.

The marital problem foreshadows the involutional problem. I am speaking of psychological, rather than endocrinological, involution, although they often go together. In people with a precarious and rigid adjustment, who have previously walked on a straight and narrow path because of fear of becoming involved in psychological catastrophe, involutional problems are particularly apt to arise. They may, however, arise even among those whose adjustment seems by conventional standards to be good. In our culture extraversion is the favored role, expecially for men. Hence, introverts very frequently take up an extraverted role because that is the way to prestige and wealth. Even an extravert may develop a need for introversion later in life. Since this need for introversion is not apt to be recognized in our society, a man or woman may feel a general vague sense of frustration, emptiness, and restlessness, despite external reasons for happiness.

These problems occur more frequently now than they used to, partly because of the increase in the age of our population. The increased incidence may also be due to the greater freedom which women have recently gained. Jungian analysis is particularly apt to be valuable at this time of life since it encourages outlet through creative work and artistic activity, particularly in the later period of analysis after neurotic symptoms and inhibitions have been worked through.

Analytical psychology can contribute to the understanding of the psychopathology of schizophrenia, paranoia and the schizoid personality. At the time of the outbreak of schizophrenia and paranoia, the first thing that often happens is a state of inflation. The ego becomes "possessed" by one or more of the archetypal images from the collective unconscious, such as the hero or a divine figure. This inflation explains the grandiosity of many schizophrenic and paranoid patients, and also why so many of them claim to be in communication with God, Jesus or the Saints. Meanwhile, the persona has been dissolved. The unconscious image displaces it and the patient becomes psychotic. If the patient recovers from the schizophrenic or paranoid attack, the persona is restored. In some cases, as previously described, the persona may actually be stronger than before. In the majority, however, the persona returns only at the price of increased repression. Therefore, the conscious personality is more shallow after the return to sanity. The patient must divert much of his reservoir of psychic energy to guard against being again overwhelmed.

Many a schizoid personality seems in his own mind to be faced with a choice of insanity or genius. Perhaps he is a person of superior intelligence, but because of his personality, his environmental circumstances or both, he is unable to realize in action the phantasies of greatness which preoccupy him. In such cases analytical psychology may have much to offer. Jung comments as follows: (16) "Primarily unconscious content rising to the level of consciousness is a not infrequent experience. If a person can only keep a cool head, he is threatened neither by insanity nor by the curse of becoming a misunderstood genius. People in such a predicament prefer to have somebody with them. They need to feel a certain understanding and sympathy that they can share their crazy ideas with someone. This relieves them of the fear of capsizing." Though this was written some years before Rosen's account (20) of the direct treatment of schizophrenia, it illustrates a similar approach to their care. Jung goes on to say, "When the main shock of the attack is over, I always try to see what has happened. We give up the intuitive language and the symbolic terminology." When, by means of this support and the demonstration that the psychiatrist understands what the patient is going through, the acute anxiety and panic quiet down, then the second stage of treatment is entered. "We try to reduce the seemingly incomprehensible events to rational sequences and to personal or impersonal origins. We hope to assimilate the experience and to integrate it instead of repressing it. Such experiences contain just those values that were painfully lacking before."

Baynes, in "The Mythology of the Soul," (1) spoke of the renegade tendency in many schizophrenics and also in many alcoholics and psychopathic personalities: that is, the tendency to want to get away from the conventional demands of society. He said that oftentimes in trying to help such cases with psychotherapy, he had the feeling that he was not talking to the whole personality. A certain renegade element stood to one side and laughed at the analyst and at the ego, as though not really being taken in. That is one reason why treatment of these conditions is so difficult.

Analytical psychology lends itself, much more readily than Freudian psychoanalysis, to the application of religious concepts in psychotherapy. Reconciling symbols of religious origin may be valuable in psychotherapy. Insofar as the person's cultural level is suited to the type of religion in which he is brought up they contribute to mental stability. If his religious outlook contains concepts which are not suited to our present day culture, then the problem may be not easier but more difficult for him. It is then the analyst's function to help the person understand the depth of his own religious doctrines or to help him seek out new religious insights of greater value to him. Jung mentions that at one time he was able to help a Parsee back to his ancestral faith, (18) so he is not partial to any particular type of religion. The patient can, it is true, construct a religious philosophy of his own. Realizing that very few people are capable of this, Jung is quite willing to use the concepts of traditional religion wherever they seem to be relevant.

I look forward eventually either to the reconciliation of all the different schools of depth psychology, or to the forming of higher, more developed concepts which will include the present ones. When in Geneva, I visited Dr. Charles Baudoin's school of "psychopedagogy," which offers training in both Freudian and Jungian analysis. In order to get a diploma in a three year course, the student must show a proficiency in both theoretical systems and in both methods of treatment. Dr. Baudoin told me that the younger students much prefer the Freudian approach while the older students are more apt to be interested in Jung. I would like to see the same sort of thing tried in this country, with the doors open for other legitimate schools of analysis. Certainly we need a great deal more study concerning the applicability of the theories and methods of Jungian analysis in psychiatry and in the psychology of individual and cultural growth.

The theories and methods of treatment of Jung should be especially valuable to those who are working with people with a genuinely religious background. An Episcopal bishop once told me that when clergymen or theological students in his diocese seemed to need psychiatric help he was reluctant to refer them to most psychiatrists, because he felt that proper account would not be taken of their religious needs and problems. Clergymen who wish to refer parishioners whom they know to have deep and sincere religious convictions would have the same reluctance. Many adolescents struggle over conflicts between genuine ideals and their natural desires. Many middle-aged people cannot live abundant lives because of inhibitions which are oppressively confining but which they dare not cast off entirely. Other persons are not ill, but are seeking ways to develop their personalities beyond the levels prescribed by the conventions of their culture. To the needs of all these sufferers and seekers Jung offers help and stimulating ideas, through an outlook substantially different from that of any other leader in psychiatric thought. It is hoped that this introduction will encourage further reading, and further original thought in the directions where Jung has pioneered.

References Cited

(See also: "Reading List" on page 81)

(1) Baynes, H. G. Mythology of the Soul. Bailliere, Tindall and Cox, London. 1940. Republished by Methuen. 1949.

(2) Brill, A. A. The only or favorite child in adult life. N. Y. State Jour. of Med. 12:463. 1912.

(3) Freud, Sigmund History of the Psychoanalytic Movement. Collected Papers, Vol. I. Hogarth Press and The Institute of Psychoanalysis, London. 1924.

(4) __________ Collected Papers, Vol. III. Hogarth Press and The Institute of Psychoanalysis, London. 1924.

(5) __________ Basic Writings of Sigmund Freud. Ed. by A. A. Brill. Modern Library. 1938.

(6) __________ Moses and Monotheism. A. Knopf, New York. 1939.

(7) __________ The Interpretation of Dreams. Macmillan Co., New York. 1942.

(8) Gray, Horace Brother Klaus by C. G. Jung; with a translation of Jung's commentary. Jour. of Nervous and Mental Diseases, 103:359. 1946.

(9) Haggard, H. Rider She. Longmans, Green, New York and London. 1907.

(10) Jacobi, Jolande The Psychology of C. G. Jung. Rev. Ed. Yale Univ. Press, New Haven. 1951.

(11) Jellinek, Augusta Spontaneous imagery–a new psychotherapeutic approach. Amer. Jour. of Psychotherapy, 3:372. 1949.

(12) Jung, C. G. The Transformations and Symbols of the Libido. transl, into English as Psychology of the Unconscious, Dodd, Mead, New York. 1912.

(13) ___________ The Psychology of Occult Phenomena. in Collected Papers on Analytical Psychology, Moffat Yard, New York. 1917.

(14) ___________ Contributions to Analytical Psychology. Harcourt, Brace, New York. 1928.

(15) ___________ Psychology of Dementia Praecox. Nervous and Mental Disease Pub. Co., New York, and Washington. 1936.

(16) ___________ The Integration of the Personality. Farrar and Rinehart, New York. 1939.

(17) ___________ Die Psychologie der Uebertragung. Rascher, Zurich. 1940.

(18) ___________ Psychologie und Alchemie. Rascher, Zurich. 1944.

(19) Maeder, Alphonse Concerning the function of dreams. Jahrbuch für psychoanalytische und psychopathologische Forschungen. 4:692. 1912.

(20) Rosen, John N. Method of resolving acute catatonic excitement. Psychiatric Quart. 20:183. 1946.

(21) Silberer, Herbert Problems of Mysticism and Its Symbolism. Translated by Smith Ely Jelliffe, Moffat Yard, New York. 1917.

(22) Storch, Alfred Primitive Archaic Forms of Inner Experience and Thought in Schizophrenia. Nervous and Mental Disease Pub. Co., New York. 1924.

(23) Wells, H. G. The Sea-Lady. 5th ed., Methuen, London. 1925.

Reading List

Books on Analytical Psychology in English:

Adler, Gerhart Studies in Analytical Psychology. Routledge and Kegan Paul, London, 1948. A clearly written series of essays with excellent case studies as well as general ones on theory, by the present director of the London Institute.

Baynes, H. G. Mythology of the Soul. Bailliere, Tindall and Cox, London, 1940. Republished by Methuen, 1949. An exhaustive study of two cases, with much technical psychiatric and mythological matter, illustrated with many paintings and drawings.

__________ Analytical Psychology and the English Mind. Methuen, London, 1950. A series of essays on theory and dream psychology, by the late leader of analytical psychology in England.

Fordham, Michael The Life of Childhood. Kegan Paul, London, 1944. Theoretical and practical considerations in the psychotherapy of children, with case illustrations, of moderate technicality.

Harding, M. Esther The Way of All Women. Longmans Green, New York, 1933. A semi-popular exposition of the psychological problems of women; by a leading New York analytical psychologist.

__________ Women's Mysteries. Longmans Green, New York, 1935. A sequel to the preceding, more technical and with more mythological material.

________________ Psychic Energy. Pantheon Books, New York, 1947. A clear presentation of analytical theory, with illustrations from cases and dreams.

Hinkle, Beatrice M. The Re-creating of the Individual. Harcourt, Brace, New York, 1923. The pioneer work in America on Jung's psychology, based largely on the "Psychological Types."

Hoop, van der, J. H. Character and the Unconscious. Harcourt, Brace, New York, 1923. A comparison of Freud's and Jung's doctrines by a leading Dutch psychiatrist.

________________ Conscious Orientation. Harcourt, Brace, 1939. A discussion of the psychological types, with much original material and theory.

Jacobi, Jolande The Psychology of C. G. Jung. (revised edition), Yale U. Press, New Haven, 1951. A condensation of Jung's theories, very complete, without case studies but illustrated with reproductions of patient's paintings, by a member of the faculty of the Jung Institute in Zurich.

Jung, C. G. The Psychology of Dementia Praecox. Nervous and Mental Disease Publishing Co., New York and Washington, 1936. The pioneer application of the association test and Freudian theory to the understanding of this baffling psychiatric illness.

__________ Psychology of the Unconscious. Dodd, Mead, New York, 1942. An interpretation of a young woman's fantasies in the light of psychology and mythology.

__________ Collected Papers on Analytical Psychology. Moffat, Yard, New York, 1917. Miscellaneous essays from Jung's earlier period, before, during and shortly after his association with Freud.

___________ *Psychological Types*. Harcourt, Brace, New York, 1924. A complete exposition of the types, together with much concerning religion, mythology, and the psychology of individuation.

___________ *Contributions to Analytical Psychology*. Harcourt, Brace, New York, 1928. Essays on the theory of analytical psychology and the female psyche.

___________ *Two Essays on Analytical Psychology*. Dodd, Mead, New York, 1928. Out of print and practically unobtainable–unfortunately so, since this is a very clear and brief presentation, with excellent case illustrations.

___________ and Richard Wilhelm *The Secret of the Golden Flower*. Kegan Paul, London, 1931. Translation of an ancient Chinese mystical text, with its implications for modern psychotherapy.

___________ *Modern Man in Search of A Soul*. Harcourt, Brace, New York, 1933. Essays on psychotherapy, the psychology of dreams, and religion.

___________ *Psychology and Religion*. Yale U. Press, New Haven, 1938. Lectures delivered at Yale University, with examples from a dream series; fairly technical.

___________ *The Integration of the Personality*. Farrar and Rinehart, New York, 1939. Essays on the psychology of dreams, alchemy, and psychotherapy.

___________ *Essays on Contemporary Events*. Kegan Paul, London, 1947. Excursions into the psychology of European politics, before, during and after the second World War.

__________ and C. Kerenyi. Essays on a Science of Mythology. Pantheon Books, New York, 1949. An inquiry into the archetype of the eternal child, with much technical mythological material.

Jung, C. G. Foreword to Introduction to Zen Buddhism, by D. T. Suzuki. Philosophical Library, New York, 1949. The 21 pages in the foreword are an excellent essay on the psychology of mysticism.

Layard, John The Lady of the Hare. Faber and Faber, London, 1944. A case in psychotherapy, and its interpretation through the mythology of the moon.

Schaer, Hans Religion and the Cure of Souls in Jung's Psychology. Pantheon Books, New York, 1950. An excellent summary of analytical psychology's relation to religion, by a Swiss pastor and lecturer at the Jung Institute in Zurich.

Wickes, Frances The Inner World of Childhood, D. Appleton, New York, 1930. A pioneer work on the analytical psychology and psychotherapy of children, in an optimistic vein, by a leading New York analyst.

__________ The Inner World of Man. H. Holt, New York, 1948. The analytical psychology of adults, with reproductions of many paintings by patients.

The Bollingen Foundation of New York is sponsoring a new complete edition of Jung's works. These are to be published in the course of the next few years by Pantheon Books, Inc. New York 14, N. Y., uniform with Essays on a Science of Mythology. Many have not been translated before.

[redacted]

[redacted]